Carol Klein

Life in a
Cottage Garden

With photographs by
Jonathan Buckley

BBC BOOKS

CONTENTS

Introduction

When we came to Glebe Cottage 32 years ago it looked a bit different from the way it looks today. It was strewn with old cars and sheds, lots of them. Now it's full of paths and walls, terraces and flower borders. There is a little pond, there are fruit and vegetable beds and a woodland garden. And it's full of plants. It's bounded by a native hedge that we planted. Each year the whole garden is the scene of an unfolding drama. There is comedy, suspense and intrigue too, and occasionally tragedy.

It's exciting, beguiling and ever-changing. It changes day by day and as each season unfolds, drifting gently or arriving urgently. Within a single day the garden can go through a hundred subtle nuances.

During the past three decades I've cared for it, giving it as much love as I could, whenever I could. It is a privilege to live here and work in this beautiful place, surrounded on all sides by the rough and ready North Devon countryside. Glebe Cottage is only 15 miles from the coast so we're subject to all the vagaries of an Atlantic climate. We have gales, huge skies, incredible cloud formations. There is no hiding from it. Sometimes there is baking sun, at other times deep snow.

There are happenings, events too. The day the first swallows arrive, gallivanting round the blue spring sky, and when they have left for their winter sojourn in far and distant lands in the south. From the north come our cold-weather visitors, flocks of redwings and fieldfares chattering across the bare fields, gathering exhausted in the huge ash tree by the house. In the morning they breakfast on berries, stripping rowan and hawthorn, fortifying themselves for their onward journey.

There are the first beech leaves opening and the last red leaf dangling from the acer.

We share the garden with a tide of creatures who have contributed for generations to its life and our enjoyment of it. There are other worlds too that play an equally vital part in my garden's life, many of them invisible to the naked eye. In the soil billions of micro-organisms play their part in giving it life and helping the garden thrive.

But the more you garden the more you realise that all that happens is a tiny instant in a huge and ongoing narrative — backwards and forwards in time. The ferns growing between the stones of the walls I built are identical to ferns that inhabited primeval swamps. The stone to build the walls was laid down millions of years ago and in its very recent history was masoned by local men to fashion walls and dwellings, some of them now disappeared.

This is the story of a year in the life of my garden.

1

January

The year starts austere, cold, uninviting. Yet there are a few more minutes of daylight than there were just days ago, when the sun reached the nadir of its annual journey during the winter solstice, and already there is a tinge of hope, a murmur deep down that suggests that this is a beginning, not an end. The way one season turns into another is inexorable, but now there is no argument; it is winter's turn and it grips the garden with strong, cold hands.

Then there is snow.

Leaden skies can make midday feel like night. There is an ominous blackness to the sky that can mean nothing but snow, and with it an inevitability – dread, but excitement too. As flakes fall thick and fast, the garden becomes invisible, the air is filled with powdery snow blown in great eddies and flurries that obliterate horizontals and verticals. A beleaguered blackbird sits incredulous on a branch fast turning white.

A bright, crisp dawn reveals the garden in its new apparel. Shape and structure are simplified under a snowy coat and the garden takes on an integrity unmatched in any

Life in a Cottage Garden

other month. Suddenly there is sculpture; the box hedge becomes a solid structure, clumps of evergreen euphorbias take on fantastic forms. All is clean and new, all blemishes and faults disappear, and an other-worldly quiet descends.

Snow sticks to paths and freezes, especially to the slate paths that dissect the west side of the garden, neatly delineating each bed. Steps too are white, and in the early morning light under a clear sky, the whiteness is imbued with apricot. This sort of light on snow, low and clear without any ferocity, generalises all the garden's features; all may look ordered, criss-crossed by pre-ordained horizontals with parallel lines enclosing neat rectangles, but all this is seen from afar. Down there, at ground level, it's a very different story.

As the snow melts throughout the garden, last year is still very much in evidence. Soil is cleggy and cold, little has been cleared and there are a hundred and one jobs to do in every small bed. Within each space there are special issues to address, and though some are common to all of them – cutting down stems or pulling away detritus from the crown of a plant to give its new buds a fighting chance – there are a multitude of tasks that have their own patterns and procedures.

Some days are dank and dark but even foggy mornings have their own January magic. As I walk through the garden, trees appear from the gloom then melt away.

Resolutions were made as January began, so before its end some of them at least must become reality.

WEDNESDAY 6 JANUARY

Frost and fierce winds have stripped the garden. Apart from the sensuous, curvy box hedges and a few evergreens and conifers, the garden is skeletal. Many perennials have died down and now the garden takes on a stark simplicity. Tree branches are exposed, unclad, the leaves that gave them their soft summer shape have fallen and their underlying structure is uncovered.

In the case of deciduous trees, it is almost like discovering their souls, their true identities. The *Cornus controversa* 'Variegata' that has grown into the focus of attention in Alice's garden is leafless but equally beautiful now in its most elemental form. The intricate structure of its twigs seems woven into a series of ascending plateaux.

Though the trees in my garden will outlast me, there will be deaths amongst other plants. Right now I am feeling the loss of my beautiful *Eryngium pandanifolium*, whose towering stems were a monument in previous winters.

There are elements of silver here and there as in the seedheads of *Miscanthus sinensis*. Though snow and rain reduced them to rats' tails, when the sun shines their fluffy flower heads recover and make an entertaining diversion and their tall stems a statuesque contribution to the bones of the winter garden.

ABOVE *It's always exciting to see who has been hopping around. Perhaps one set of tracks was made by the cock blackbird now sitting on a low branch of the eleagnus.*
OPPOSITE *We do not always have snow in January, but when we do it changes everything; the whole garden becomes a snowstorm.*

It is cold and wild and hostile. There is no sympathy from it; 'take it or leave it', it seems to say.

Most of the weather here is from the West, it's Atlantic weather and though we are miles from the ocean, with Exmoor between us to the North and ridges and river valleys to the West, when gales bite home you can taste the salt if you run your finger down the window glass and lick it.

We are high above the sea here, about 600 feet, and though there is a little wood adjacent to the garden and far too many trees within it that we have planted since we came here, thirty years ago, nonetheless the garden feels open and in the midst of winter, very exposed. Although, still the trunks and branches are encrusted with lichen, a reminder of milder times.

FRIDAY 15 JANUARY

Somehow you don't expect your nostrils to be assailed by scent on a cold winter's day; it's probably for that reason that winter scent is so memorable. There are only a few shrubs in my garden whose perfume pervades the air in January, but they are enough to scent the whole garden. The witch hazel came into flower well before Christmas but its spidery flowers are still pumping out their perfume; they're joined now by the long dangling bells of *Mahonia japonica*. Close your eyes and, but for your tingling fingertips and your cold nose, it could be May. The flowers of this lovely evergreen shrub have the identical scent to muguet, lily-of-the-valley.

At the beginning of the year any flowers tough enough to show their faces last for months, and so too does their scent. Their strategy in flowering at this inhospitable time of year is to ensure pollination. Though there are few insects around now, those that are on the wing make a beeline for any flower with scent. So – fewer pollinators, but fewer competitors. As you walk up the track, the scent from a tall, dense *Viburnum* x *bodnantense* stops you in your tracks. At first it's difficult to pinpoint where the scent comes from; the flowers are tiny, gathered together in small clusters. Even when you can't see them at all, as dusk descends you can still enjoy their sweet, honeyed scent. It seems to follow you as you make your way back into the warmth of the cottage.

WEDNESDAY 20 JANUARY

When the snow melts there's a new perfume in the air – or at least a new smell. Suddenly you're aware of the soil, so long out of sight and out of mind under its thick white covering, and I'm reminded that far from being dead, life has been going on underneath its crisp white surface. Everywhere the new spears of snowdrops are starting to appear, and some of them are having to make their way through soil that was raked and scraped way back in autumn. It's time to move in with the leaf mould and make them welcome.

ABOVE *Several of the small-flowered species asters have another incarnation long after their flowers have faded. When their fluffy seed heads have parachuted away, they leave these shimmering stars behind.* OPPOSITE *The tiered framework of* Cornus controversa *'Variegata' is laid bare.*

Life in a Cottage Garden

FRIDAY 22 JANUARY

The snow has lulled me into a false sense of security; after all, it's impossible to work at ground level when the whole garden's white. But my task for today isn't at ground level, it's way up in the air amongst the branches of my beloved crab apple. It's called 'Golden Hornet' and as well as being smothered in blossom in May its glowing amber fruit stretches right into the winter. It plays host to *Clematis* 'Huldine', a vigorous *viticella* cultivar that bears white starry flowers with mother-of-pearl reverses. To call it vigorous is to understate the case; instead of embellishing the branches of the crab apple in a decorous way, it's trying to take over. Now in midwinter it looks for all the world like a giant bird's nest, like a Quentin Blake creation. But this is no laughing matter – the well-being of the crab apple is at stake. This enormous bundle of twiggy growth is gradually pushing the branches of the crab apple apart and I must come to its rescue. Neil's volunteered to hold the ladder, and up I go into the topmost branches. With the heftiest loppers I can wield, I chop out huge chunks of excess growth, bundling them up and throwing them to the ground – my position is precarious but Neil's is downright dangerous. Gradually, gradually order is reinstated. Although the classic way to prune *Clematis viticella* is down to a couple of buds above the ground, I'm leaving several strong shoots to clamber through the branches of the crab but spacing them out so they're more evenly distributed. I'm hoping to see in autumn branches laden with fruit and spangled with big, opalescent stars.

MONDAY 25 JANUARY

Some clearing tasks are monumental, but the best policy is to dive in as soon as the weather allows. The sere stems of grasses and perennials in the hot borders had a heightened sense of drama with a covering of snow, but as soon as it's gone their pale, dead stems lie forlornly amongst the other skeletons. In January I am always torn between tidying up for a fresh start and leaving old stems and leaves to protect the embryonic shoots that will give beds and borders their fine summer persona – and I do want to leave some of the seedheads for winter rations for the birds. However, everything in these borders is so sodden, I have no choice. Out comes barrowful after barrowful and I take them over to the compost heap, where they will play an important role. I treat most hardy herbaceous perennials the same – cutting down their stems close to ground level. There is no point my leaving stubby stems which would only rot and endanger the health of new shoots. In the case of gingers, stems often tumble after the first severe frost. I take them off and mound up soil on top of their rhizomes. The whole idea is to ensure frost cannot penetrate. It's a bit of an odd sight – rather like the scene of an invasion by giant moles – but who cares if it does the job. Earlier I ignored my own advice. I hope they're still alive – fingers crossed.

OPPOSITE Getting to grips with the hot border. It's not so hot at the moment, but there's certainly enough to do to get me warmed up.
BELOW Evidence, if any were needed, of just how cold it has been. Some of these pots are, or were, as old as our cottage.

January
Snowdrops

The first flower, and the one that epitomises January, is the snowdrop. Even those who have no interest in nature or gardening have a fondness for it and recognise it immediately, almost instinctively. It always seems to grow in close proximity to human habitation, close to old gardens and graveyards. How can something so slender be so strong? It is a masterpiece of evolutionary design. And what a strategy for survival – a bulb that can store its food when it is done and rest dormant, sleeping till the change in day length tells it that it is time to wake up.

Short shoots, emerging singly, slowly part and push the precious flower bud upwards, launching it into adolescent life. The bell emerges gradually hanging its head, big drops of pure and pristine white. As it matures, three petals part, revealing the dainty underskirts trimmed with green. The outer petals still protect the inner ones so that pollinating insects, attracted by the scent and guided by the green marks, can safely avail themselves of nectar and deposit their precious cargo of pollen. The temperature inside the flower is two degrees warmer than the ambient temperature, to protect the pollen.

The flowers are suspended on fine pedicels, the slenderest of stalks. No matter how brutal the buffeting wind or how heavy their swelling ovaries, they dance blithely, righting themselves. When they push up through snow they treat it as protection. They are cosseted by it rather than threatened.

Later, when seed is set, the weight of the capsules brings them gently to the ground. Gradually they will open, dispersing their seed. The bulb goes to sleep while other plants grow around it and the spring and summer cavalcade takes over until the earliest hours of the next new year, when the snowdrops stir once more and prepare to announce the coming of January.

In ditches, woods and hedgerows snowdrops congregate; they are sociable plants, seemingly loving each other's company. In gardens too they look best in crowds. Left to their own devices they will colonise and spread, but how wonderful to give them a helping hand. As their foliage starts to retreat back into the bulbs I dig up dense clumps, separate the bulbs and replant them each in its own planting hole up to 5 or 6 inches deep, enriching their new home with compost and leaf mould. I stagger distances between them, trying to emulate the way they would spread themselves.

For certain snowdrops, especially those in short supply or that I want to increase quickly (some would say greedily), twin-scaling is worth trying. In June or July, when the bulbs are sinking into dormancy, I dig them up, clean off the outside tunic, cut across the top of the bulb and clean up its basal plate, sitting the bulb upright. Using a sterile blade I slice straight down through the centre and continue to slice. Then the slices are prised apart gently into two-piece chunks (hence twin-scaling), each with its little piece of base plate. The pieces are lowered into a bag of damp vermiculite, the bag is sealed and placed in a warm spot with all light excluded. After a few weeks new bulbs will form at their base, when I line them out in trays of potting compost and encourage them to grow on.

OPPOSITE *Strong shoots push leaf litter aside, intent on growth. Nothing will stop them now.* BELOW *Galanthus 'S. Arnott', not only one of the most perfectly formed snowdrops, but also one of the best scented, with a soft, honeyed perfume.*

Life in a Cottage Garden

THE TOP OF THE WOODLAND PATH

An old hazel arches over the path that leads down into our woodland.
This is rather a grand title for what is in effect several trees (all planted
since we got here) with small beds around them, divided by gravel paths.
Its prime time is spring, with a succession of bulbs, hellebores and
pulmonarias. Summer is gloriously green and autumn magical with
golden cercidiphyllum, but a covering of snow in January transforms it
to somewhere magical.

2

February

February can be so cruel it makes you cry; dark, depressing, demoralising – and so cold. Yet it is also the month of anticipation, when the realisation that spring is coming first begins to sink in, as the gloom is pierced suddenly by shafts of golden sunlight. Or was that just a mirage – surely the whole world is stuck in an endless cycle of cold, rain, sleet and snow and thrashing, ear-aching wind? February can be so chilly that all I want to do is retire, hibernate in the cottage and cuddle up with Neil and our animals.

Sometimes frost can be so penetrating it makes me recoil each time I plunge my hands into the debris that lies in frozen layers in anarchic tangles across beds and borders, the frost fusing stems and leaves to each other and to the ground on which they lie. Perhaps it would be better to wait, maybe new shoots shouldn't be laid bare – but there is so much to do. Positively, there is huge satisfaction from pushing barrowful after barrowful of inanimate, colourless detritus to the compost heap. Central to all the activity in the garden, this process of transformation from life to death to life again never ceases to amaze and thrill me.

ABOVE AND OPPOSITE
Lichen abounds throughout our garden, decorating branches and benches. If I stood still long enough it would probably grow on me too.

Life in a Cottage Garden

Though all of it is explicable in scientific terms, that does not take away any of the magic or wonderment.

The light in the garden at Glebe Cottage is enchanting. Because the land is south-facing and sloping, we experience the whole gamut of special effects. We are treated to a constantly changing light show, never the same twice. Early in the morning light streams in from the east, filtered through the trunks of gnarled old oaks. At this time of year they are leafless and they stand silhouetted against the cold new dawn. Some days the light is soft, bathing mossy banks and tree branches embossed with lichen in its even glow. In the late afternoon, for this is when the sun sets, all is imbued with a warm glow. But the sun sets early and then temperatures plummet.

Evidence of the cruelty of winter is all around. Pots are shattered, their contents spilling forth as the thaw begins then are frozen once more in suspended animation. Wattle fences have become completely rickety; buffeted and battered by the wind, they almost fall apart as you look on. More importantly, so many plants have succumbed. The worst affected seem to be those with linear leaves, especially those from the Antipodes and South America. Most of my libertias have become casualties and the handsome astelias, for so long the centrepiece of one bed on the shady side of the garden, are past saving.

Though weather from the west predominates in Devon, in February there are some days when the sky grows sullen and menacing and you know something is about to change. The wind swings round to the east and the garden begins to shiver. This is the cruellest wind; my mum called it a lazy wind – one that instead of going round you goes straight through you.

I begin to yearn for March. There are hazel catkins in the hedge and the pussy willow has begun to change from silver to gold; it can't be far away.

Friday 5 February

I never stop sowing seeds, but now that daylight hours are a little longer and there is an occasional optimistic hint of warmth in the air, seed sowing begins in earnest. Anything tender and annual has to take priority. If it's to do its sub-tropical best it needs as long a season as possible.

Years ago, our youngest daughter Alice and I collected seed from a particularly dark ricinus 'tree' on a piece of waste ground in Greece. That's to say, I collected the seed and Alice watched in deep embarrassment. This is a castor oil plant, whose huge palmate leaves give a dramatic twist to our hot beds. The seeds themselves look alien – beans with seedcoats netted and marbled like shells picked up from a tropical beach. They have maintained their viability and produced crop after crop of exotic plants capable of reaching several feet in one season. The ricinus seeds are big, and I push each one into its own separate compartment in a module tray. They would be quite happy to be sown immediately into individual pots.

ABOVE *Station sowing – sowing individually and giving each seed its own space, is ideal for the big beans of* Ricinus communis, *the castor-oil plant.*
OPPOSITE *Though they're obscured by fallen leaves, it's worth rooting around to cut old fern fronds right down to their bases.*

Ricinus are highly poisonous but I am sowing edible plants in exactly the same way. A broad bean and beetroot salad is a late-spring treat, and though broad beans can be sown in late autumn, I never do this. The soil in my vegetable garden is too heavy. Sown in toilet-roll middles filled with good compost, each one has the best possible chance not only of germinating, but of growing away strongly, so that in less than a month they are big enough to plant out.

Some seedlings, though, will need a little more nurture. This year I'd love to have quantities of white cosmos and mahogany rudbeckia to enrich and reinforce colour schemes around the garden. I'm sowing *Cosmos bipinnatus* 'Purity' and *Rudbeckia hirta* 'Rustic Dwarfs'. Both are members of the daisy family, Asteraceae, though each creates a very different effect. The seeds are similar, though – long and narrow. In fact another family member, coreopsis, is called tickseed. I sprinkle the seed finely on the surface of compost in half trays, cover it with grit, and press the whole caboodle down firmly with a made-to-measure presser board that Neil fashioned many moons ago.

SUNDAY 7 FEBRUARY

In 1999 we made a garden at the Chelsea Flower Show. I had already been exhibiting at all the major shows for the previous ten years, but this was my very first time creating a show garden. Its ethos was that it would sustain and regenerate itself, and at its hub was a potting shed/greenhouse designed and constructed by Neil, which has morphed into my current potting shed. It is in constant use, but it's on cold February days like today that it really comes into its own. What a good job there is electric light here so activities can be continued long after dark. Neil's old work bench has become the centrepiece and it's the crux in more ways than one; practically all the plants I grow from seeds and cuttings start their life on this bench, some of them returning several times to be pricked out and potted on before finally taking up residence in the garden.

SATURDAY 13 FEBRUARY

Propagation is one of my favourite parts of gardening, but in February opportunities are limited – weather and temperature conspire against it. But it's at this time traditionally that one kind of propagating is best carried out. As soon as the day warms up a little, I get wrapped up and take my tools down to Annie's garden, where large clumps of poppies are already showing their bright green rosettes in contrast to the dun appearance of the rest of the bed. It's not the foliage that I'm interested in, though; I want to extract some nice healthy roots from which I can take root cuttings.

There are two ways of doing this: either I can dig up a whole plant and carry it off triumphantly to my shed, or I can dig down the side of the plant

ABOVE Iris 'Katharine Hodgkin' is quite unique, ice blue and decorated with dark blue abstract patterns. The stems adjust their length to push the flowers through the snow. OPPOSITE What a treat to repot these huge Eucomis 'Sparkling Burgundy'. New shoots are already emerging.

Life in a Cottage Garden

and sever a few big, chunky roots. The roots are laid out on the table or bench, ensuring that the cut ends closest to the crown of the plant are uppermost. Each root will make several cuttings, but each piece must be planted the same way up. I never bother with distinguishing top and bottom ends by making a sloping cut at the bottom end, as most books advise; as long as I plant them straightaway, I know which end is which. Each piece is pushed into a separate module so that its top is just flush with the compost. I sprinkle grit over the surface of the tray, water thoroughly and place the tray onto a heated bench in the greenhouse. It won't be long before the new shoots start to appear.

Saturday 20 February

Both our daughters have their own gardens, though they are 'Annie and Alice's gardens' in name rather than because they play an active role in looking after them! Nonetheless, the girls are both very fond of the whole garden, and in particular their designated borders. Alice's garden has undergone a few changes since its inception, but Annie's is in dire need of some rejuvenation and a fresh approach – nothing too revolutionary in terms of design, as both perimeters and parameters are clearly established. It must fit in seamlessly, and yet replanting must give it more order and at the same time a generous helping of vivacity.

Any bed or border is in danger of losing its way unless it has constant attention and ongoing thought. In a herbaceous planting, big, buxom characters tend to take over, crowding out less bumptious individuals and often special plants are lost in the free-for-all.

It isn't a question of out with the old, in with the new, but an attempt to re-use the best plants and replant them in a different way, meanwhile adding fresh plants to create new pictures. I even have a rough plan on paper, though the one in my head, imagining how things will look and what will follow what, refines itself constantly as I see what I have to work with and as I try out new ideas.

Today, work starts in earnest. The weather has held up proceedings and the whole bed had to be covered in tarpaulin in a vain attempt to keep my heavy soil dry enough to work on. Eventually the rain stops, but now the tarpaulin comes out again, spread right along the path that divides the girls' gardens. Fifi decides this is a new game specially invented just for her entertainment. It's good bicep-building work, as clump after clump is lifted from the cold and heavy soil, divided into healthy sections with the old woody centres of plants discarded, then stacked along the path until it fills it all and has to be accommodated round the corner and on every nearby step.

Some plants will find their way to a nursery bed, some will be divided and potted to be used in other parts of the garden. It's a lot to do, but at least with damp weather nothing is liable to dry out.

OPPOSITE *It is a thrilling proposition that these chunks of root will become strong plants before the year is out.*
BELOW *Fifi, our new puppy, is just about three months old. She happily surveys the garden from the warmth of my duffle coat.*

February

Hellebores

....

What is it about hellebores that makes them so alluring?

Part of it is to do with when they put on their best show. Perhaps if they flowered in the midst of the summer display they might go unnoticed. They are not tall plants, and none could ever be accused of being flamboyant. Their 'flowers' are composed of sepals rather than petals; these last for months and eventually all fade to a subtle green. The range of colour when they are in flower is staggering; from immaculate white to virtually black and in between through pinks, purples, clarets, yellows and greens. Some have the subtlety of a wood pigeon's breast, others the depth and strength of rich red wine.

These plants hang their heads demurely so that all we see at first is the back of their flowers. This is what makes them so mysterious and unpredictable. Half their charm is this secrecy and everyone who grows hellebores understands the joy of gently turning up their flowers to appreciate the subtleties within. Sometimes there are spots and blotches arranged in symmetrical patterns, sometimes subtle shading with perhaps a picotee edge. At their centre all have a breathtaking arrangement of nectaries and a boss of golden stamens topped with pollen-rich anthers which makes them easy plants to cross. There is no time like the present!

It's only worth trying it if you start with two really top-notch plants. The black lid of a biro rubbed smartly on my jeans produces static that allows me to pick up pollen efficiently, and can be washed and dried if I want to make more than one cross. Using this lid, I take the pollen either direct from an open flower or, if I want to make sure its pollen is fluffy and potent, I float the flower in shallow water overnight indoors. However I collect pollen, it is dabbed onto the anthers of a flower on the mother plant by carefully opening a fat, virgin bud and depositing the collected pollen onto the central stigma. I close the petals and, if possible, repeat the process on three separate days. Sunny days are best, but at this time of the year three consecutive sunny days might be too much to hope for! Once pollinated, I loosely tie a bit of coloured wool (I use my grandma's embroidery silks) behind the flower and stick a bit of the same wool onto the page of a notebook and make a careful record of both parents alongside. Come late May or early June there should be fat pods full of seed and there will be a record of how each cross was made.

I try to catch seed before it falls to the ground, sowing it straightaway on the surface of gritty, loam-based seed compost, covering it with grit, watering from underneath and leaving the pots outside. The pots can be covered to protect seeds from the predations of mice; I'll check regularly, and when the first seed leaves start to emerge, I'll remove any covering. When seedlings develop a few leaves, I separate them and prick them out into individual pots. Potting them on regularly produces sturdy little plants.

When it's time for my new seedlings to face the big wide world, I plant them out in dappled shade. It will often take two, or even three, years before they flower, but when they do, I'll keep those that show star quality.

ANNIE'S GARDEN

It's hard to believe that just about everything, with the exception of the apple and crab apple, the roses and a few camassias, was taken out of Annie's border and laid along the path on a tarpaulin in February. After replanting using plenty of home-made compost, the bed burgeoned. Leafy and green in May, by the end of June it was full of flowers, and as September arrived it looked as if it had been planted for years.

3

March

March sounds a clarion call. The garden stretches itself, waking from its slumbers. Underneath the soil's cold surface there may have been ceaseless activity throughout the long winter but above ground the wakening is gradual. Only towards the end of the month does it begin to crank up. Some days can be so cold that it feels as though the garden has changed its mind, yawned, pulled up the covers and fallen asleep again. Each time it wakes up, though, it is for longer and its urge to get on with it is stronger.

All winter long, tree buds have been swelling. They are fat now, pregnant with new flower, for it is tree flowers that are first on the scene, adorning bare branches. The embryonic buds of my two magnolias were already visible when the last of their golden leaves fluttered to the ground in November. This year's flowers are encased in furry coats, eminently strokable, like so many small creatures living in the branches. For months they have been growing away, increasing imperceptibly until now when, on sunny days (for there are such days in March), they open in quick succession. In the hedgerows hazel catkins tumble out of fat

ABOVE AND OPPOSITE
Spring plants are irrepressible; whether it's trilliums in the woodland or self-sown celandines flowering blatantly in the crevices between the risers on the stone steps up to the kitchen.

Life in a Cottage Garden

buds, eager to spread their pollen, and pussy willow join them, also decorated with golden pollen.

Hazel and pussy willow are the two most iconic catkin bearers. Every child should have the opportunity to shake the hazel's lambs' tails and feel the sleek, silver catkins of the pussy willow against their cheek.

Leaf buds are changing, too, and though it will be two months before our beeches burst into vernal growth, their buds are swelling and changing colour day by day. From the house the long run of beeches that lines the lower part of our track has taken on a different caste, pink and promising, replacing their dun wintry persona, but some precocious leaves are risking it. It is always impossible to choose which new tree leaves best evoke the spirit of spring's newness, but those of cercidiphyllum have to be one of the primary contenders. They are tiny now, bronze and so translucent you can almost see through them, especially when they are up above your head against a bright spring sky.

There comes a day in March when you know the tug-of-war between winter and spring is over; spring wins the day, the balance is tipped. The coming of the vernal equinox may formalise the issue but the proof of the pudding is more visceral; the smell of newly turned soil, the first whiff of primrose, the feel of compost between your fingers, crumbly and co-operative and waiting to get going.

Wintry days become a memory and the sounds, sights and smells of spring take over.

Everywhere shoots are beginning to emerge; plants make their entrance in various ways and it is at this early stage that their individuality is most obvious. By the time summer spreads itself their esoteric natures are subsumed into the multi-coloured melee; right now they rejoice in their own unique personalities.

The scarlet buds of *Geranium psilostemon,* just discernible amongst clumps of fading snowdrops, are the essence of the plant to come. One glimpse and the picture of them in magnificent maturity – big, green, palmate leaves overlooked by masses of brilliant magenta flowers – flashes before my eyes.

Friday 5 March

If the primrose was a new introduction from some far-off place, gardeners would fight each other to possess it. Perfect pale flowers with an egg-yolk centre held on stems the colour of baby birds above rosettes of dark, crinkled leaves, the primula epitomises the coming of spring.

Essentially an edge-of-woodland plant, along with man the primrose has moved out to the banks and ditches he has created. In the countryside around Glebe Cottage, hedgerows are alive with its pallid flowers and, on a sunny day, the air is filled with their sweet scent, available just where it is needed – at nose level.

Self-sown plants always put themselves in the right place. No matter how carefully you place them they never look quite so apt as when they make up their own minds. OPPOSITE *Our native primrose is at home amongst oak leaves and ferns while* BELOW *a pale-flowered* Hepatica triloba *nestles at the foot of a rock.*

In its natural habitat it seeds itself around, each new plant becoming an established clump, spreading out gradually in search of nutrients amongst the debris of leaves and moss. Initially in the garden, though, it needs a helping hand. It is a sociable plant and always looks at its best in colonies.

When we first moved here I bought one plant, and from that lone individual we now have banks of primroses. I like to think that if and when the garden sinks back into nature, these primroses will feel so much at home they will continue to spread themselves around.

Meanwhile, it is great fun to make more. Though our primroses will seed themselves it is so easy to supplement their ranks it has almost become a ritual to grow them each year from seed. I collect it not when the seed capsule has turned brown and dry but when it is fat to bursting but still green. One seedpod may make fifty or so new plants. I sever the pod from the plant and with sharp thumbnails split its tight transparent membrane and push out the brilliant-green seeds within onto the surface of a tray of seed compost. They may need a little persuasion since they are so new and fresh that they sometimes stick together. Gradually I wipe them across the compost, then cover them with a thin layer of grit to push them into close contact with the soil. When I've watered them, by standing the pots or trays in a shallow bowl of water, they can be left outside until they germinate – usually within a matter of weeks. It is quite a thrill to see a green mist cover the top of the compost and to look on as the percentage of green increases, almost covering the surface of the tray. When seedlings have developed their first true leaves they can be pricked out. If they are big enough I move them on into individual pots and plant them out either in the autumn or in the following spring.

WEDNESDAY 10 MARCH

It's a satisfying feeling to take a broad rake and run it across the border under the *Acer palmatum* 'Osakazuki', collecting the last of the debris. Finally I'm bidding the winter farewell, and as stems and decayed leaves lift away from the soil in mats, its surface is revealed and countless tiny green shoots and the close-knotted crowns of perennials and ferns are laid bare. It is now that my obsessional tendencies come to the fore. If there is time after I've carried away the harvest of this rough but effective clearing of the ground to the compost heap, I'm down on my knees and in amongst it, removing any remaining detritus, trimming the remnants of old stalks still protruding from the ground and generally making the whole place as pristine as possible.

My garden is not carefully organised with a place for everything and everything in its place, far from it, but in March there is a serious effort to spring-clean. It's not just a ritual, it's important to enable bulbs and new shoots to break through without hindrance and later, when these beds are

ABOVE *March sunshine encourages the first optimistic shoots of* Narcissus triandrus. *Soon there will be bumpy buds and, later still, deliciously scented white flowers.*
OPPOSITE *Call me superficial, but my favourite clearing-up jobs are those that make a visual difference — even if it is cosmetic. I love raking leaves.*

Life in a Cottage Garden

mulched with dark compost, the stage will be ready for all the performers in the spring and summer show that follows.

I'm careful to avoid big clumps of *Galanthus* 'S. Arnott'. They are still hanging on – everything is off to a slow start this year and on this, one of the first sunny days in March, with the shadow of the acer traced across the now bare ground, the honey scent from this most perfumed of snowdrops fills the clear air. I'm smiling.

FRIDAY 12 MARCH

The near-black flowers of *Fritillaria persica* 'Adiyaman' are breathtaking. They don't arrive until late April but the big, fat, hollow bulbs with their alluring foxy smell that I potted up last October have launched their fat shoots. For months there is no sign of them, then one day the first shoot is there and rapidly the others push through the compost. There is a point at which you want to say 'Stop!'; they are so new, so perfect and covered in a grape-like bloom that I don't want to touch them for fear of spoiling it. They are almost rude in their insistence; nothing will stop them and their shoots extend almost before my very eyes.

SUNDAY 14 MARCH

The shadowy space under shrubs or trees often cries out for something light to add a bit of sparkle, so years ago I planted *Astelia chathamica* in one of the small woodland beds towards the top of the garden. It is a big, handsome clump of a plant with long, sword-like leaves, each elegantly arched and terminating in a sharp, definite point. These are ridged and completely silver, but white on their reverse.

Although it has been seized upon as a statement plant by garden designers and put to frequent use among gravel and boulders in sunny scenarios, it is essentially a plant of dappled shade. It also prefers a soil that doesn't dry out, so I thought it would be ideal in the spot I gave it. It was, and it grew to substantial proportions, but then we had a hard winter followed by another one. Despite every effort to resuscitate it, it was finally declared dead.

Today Neil is giving me a hand to dig it out, and when the remains of the astelia are unceremoniously dumped on the compost heap it's time to plant its replacement. We've chosen an amelanchier called 'La Paloma' – 'The Dove'. These North American trees are splendid subjects for small gardens and though our garden is bigger than some, there isn't much space left. The soil is still cleggy but we've got a barrowful of compost to help, and on this side of the garden underneath the heavy clay there is shillet (the local term for shale), which should help with drainage. Let's hope it settles in. There are flower buds already, so soon we should see a few of its starburst white flowers – a taste of what we can look forward to over the years to come.

OPPOSITE *Even though these* Fritillaria persica *'Adiyaman' are in pots there's no disguising their impatience to grow. Within a week tight buds turn to anxious thrusting shoots.*
BELOW *The flowers of* Amelanchier *'La Paloma' are pure white. They are accompanied by the first leaves, all rusty red. In summer there is a green lull, followed in September by rubescent autumn colour.*

TUESDAY 16 MARCH

The onions you grow yourself always taste better and keep better than those you buy from the supermarket. It's time I got my onion sets into the ground – or at least on top of it! In my heavy clay soil, especially when there is always the possibility of wet weather in March (it's actually a racing certainty), they can sometimes rot, so for the last few years I've taken the precaution of planting them on the top of ridges. Because we grow all our vegetables in raised beds, we can plant them more intensively than in a traditional veg bed. I always grow from sets rather than seed. Onion sets have been heat-treated to stop them rushing into flower; it's one of those gardening shortcuts that really helps. I'm planting a red and a white variety – the red one, mild and sweet, is 'Red Baron'; the white is 'Sturon', trusted and true – and when I've made little ridges they are planted every six inches or so into the top of them. This means that roots will have the chance to grow strongly without rotting and that when eventually the bulbs put on weight they will have the opportunity to ripen, basking in the sun.

THURSDAY 18 MARCH

Things are really warming up – it's a beautiful day, ideal for putting up the new fence panels that were delivered a few days ago. The old fence that separated the nursery from the rest of the garden was rickety and we had to take down two of the panels, both in imminent danger of collapse, before they fell and smashed some of the prize hellebores and snowdrops growing at their feet. Having a fence running from east to west creates two diverse sets of conditions – shade on the north and full light on the south. The fence panels run through the centre of one enormous raised bed so the soil is the same on both sides of the divide, although it dries out far more quickly to the south, especially when the sun is hot and we have prolonged periods without rain.

There are climbers on the south side of the fence – two roses and an enormous *Vitis coignetiae* that takes off in all directions. I once watched a student at Beth Chatto's magical garden pruning an old *Vitis coignetiae* which grows against a vast wall and onto a roof behind; it is trained and pruned every year (possibly twice), when all the laterals are cut back to two buds. A painstaking operation but necessary if you need to keep this most vigorous of vines within bounds. Ours has run amok, climbing into the cercidiphyllums and the copper beech that I unwisely planted on either side of the fence. When autumn comes I never regret its wild behaviour, as its huge leaves of up to a foot across turn a kaleidoscopic range of colour from reds, oranges and scarlets to rich, vinous crimson. A few days ago, though, I cut it back severely – it would have been impossible to retrain its enormous extended stems against our new panels.

ABOVE *I'm not a dab hand with the power tools but I can manage to lend a hand with a cordless drill. These oak fence panels should last for many years.* OPPOSITE *With their roots well above the surrounding soil and their shoots eventually held high, my onion sets should do well here.*

Life in a Cottage Garden

Sunday 21 March

Though a brisk north-west wind is biting my cheeks, an exploratory tour of the garden can't be delayed any longer. Everywhere shoots are beginning to emerge. Bulbs in particular make rapid progress asserting themselves, leading the way. One day you are aware of the tips of their leaves straining against the soil, the next their shoots seem inches high. Bulbs are wondrous; all that food stored in a perfectly evolved package, drawing in extra from the soil when it needs it and bursting into leaf and flower. Almost all bulbs spend only a very short time at the height of their performance before fading away almost as rapidly as they appeared. In their native habitat they all exploit a niche – a combination of temperature, soil and habitat – to enable them to flower successfully and set seed.

A late spring has made for a long winter. The earth has seldom seemed so dank and dreary for so long, yet even the most pessimistic of gardeners cannot help but respond to the appearance of brand new shoots. They form the vanguard of the coming season. Even when it advances at a crawl, these furled leaves and fat buds instil the feeling of inexorability. Nothing can stop spring's progress.

Wednesday 24 March

Already *Euphorbia sikkimensis* has put in its first appearance. Groups of pink shoots spring up, leaves outlined and veined in bright red. We have a patch of this spurge along with clumps of *Galanthus* 'Atkinsii', a large early snowdrop, and the two make a memorable picture. Later the spurge grows to several feet. It has a rangy habit, loose and lolloping, and it looks best where it is allowed to grow in its own informal way, but right now all its beauty is concentrated into short shoots.

Friday 26 March

All peonies are arresting at an early stage, none more so than my favourite, *Paeonia* 'Late Windflower'. Its new shoots are plump and full of promise, yet sharply pointed, evolved to pierce the soil. Unfolding leaves and straight stems are spectacular, many intensely crimson. Herbaceous peonies rising through clumps of our native primrose are a springtime treat second to none. These new stems have a perfect polish, a quality shared by several other herbaceous plants at this time of year.

One of the reasons I love herbaceous plants is the way they change, going through a series of different guises throughout the time they are above ground; we are aware of different aspects of their personality at each time of the year. Right now, in the paeony's case it is these scarlet shoots that concentrate the attention. In just a few weeks they will be forgotten, pushed

OPPOSITE *Bulbs are the essence of spring; dark ground is suddenly bespangled by their bright jewels. The rapidity with which they appear has you catching your breath.* Puschkinia *var.* libanotica *is splendid, gay and unpretentious.*
BELOW *Most spurges are grown for their brilliant lime-green heads, but several have exciting young shoots, often of bright red or orange.*

into second place as its huge white flowers flaunt their fabulous petals, each bloom lit with a boss of golden anthers. Later there will be seedheads and later still, handsome, rubescent autumn foliage.

Emerging shoots and buds are to be enjoyed both in their own right and for their promise. They may not have the volume of summer's bounty but they build the anticipation of the coming season, whetting the appetite for what is to come. Spring proper is on its way.

MONDAY 29 MARCH

Dry days give me the opportunity to finish cutting back some of the stems that have been left through the winter, either because they looked good or because they supported seedheads for hungry birds. We have been feeding the birds all winter through, especially during the prolonged snow, and we will continue to do so right through the year. Any additional rations they might glean from old seedheads around the garden are minimal now. There comes a point when, however attractive stems and seedheads may have been, their time is up. Out with the old and in with the new. The old, black, bobbly heads of rudbeckia are cut back to the ground, enormous stems of fennel are given the chop with loppers, taking great care not to damage the intricate frizz of purple new growth that has sprung up in their midst. I pile up all the seedheads next to the compost heap so birds and small mammals can continue to help themselves.

Some ornamental grasses are much prized for their steadfastness when winter comes, moving noisily when fierce winds blow and standing white and hoary after a frost. But at the stage before this they often have even more to offer. The pendant golden blades of the Japanese grass *Hakonechloa macra* 'Aureola' are dipped in pink and crimson and the plain green species changes, chameleon-like, as if to fit in with the glowing garden. That is a thing of the past now – and of the future. Now they are all golden but beginning to look tatty, but they've had a good innings; ten out of twelve months isn't bad.

Both the variegated cultivar and the straight species are important plants in the brick garden. Four big plants of *Hakonechloa macra* grow in containers at the coincidence of the main paths within the garden and in the ground beside; the variegated version is confined to pots. With a pair of small, sharp shears, I'm chopping back all its old growth as close to the top of the pot as I can. The miscanthus will come in for the same treatment, their top growth has been left throughout the winter. The other important grasses in my garden – the molinias – will clean themselves. At some point, usually after a severe frost in December, their gleaming golden stems tumble to the ground in a tidy heap. I scoop them up and take them into the house to continue the show indoors. They are there still, but meanwhile, outside, their new shoots are beginning to stir. Within a few weeks they will be through.

ABOVE *Sweet pea, Lathyrus 'Cupani' seed collected from our own plants and sown only a couple of weeks ago have made headlong progress.* OPPOSITE *Shears at the ready, the hakonechloa is cut hard back. Neil sharpens my shears for me; honed cutting tools make for quick and efficient tidying up.*

Life in a Cottage Garden

March
Magnolia

Some people would say magnolias are too grand for my garden. I have to disagree. There are only two of them – a *Magnolia stellata*, the star magnolia, and *Magnolia* x *loebneri* 'Leonard Messel', which has *Magnolia stellata* as one of its parents. Both are slow growing and, which is a great advantage for an impatient gardener like me, both flower from an early age. Whereas *Magnolia stellata* spreads its branches widely, 'Leonard Messel' is more upright but probably grows taller. We shall see.

My mum lusted over *Magnolia stellata*. It is a very glamorous little tree and one of the few she could have accommodated in her tiny Manchester back garden. On a visit to Reginald Kaye's nursery in Silverdale, at the back of Morecambe Bay, we managed to acquire a small bare stick with roots in a pot whose label declared it to be *Magnolia stellata*. After a planting ceremony there was nothing to do than sit back and wait for the magical flowers eventually to appear. She waited for 15 years, by which time the magnolia had grown to such massive proportions and was covered with such huge leaves that even the most optimistic amongst us realised it was not what it should have been. Eventually it was replaced by the real thing and duly flowered two years after planting.

Meanwhile, the *Magnolia stellata* that we planted here thirty years ago had been growing apace, so at least my mum had that vicarious enjoyment. It was one of a consignment of trees and shrubs that we bought from the old Veitch's nursery, carrying them home triumphantly in the open back of our Land Rover. A place of honour was prepared for the magnolia, with the very best diet of leaf mould and compost. Each spring since it has thrilled us with its show of perfect, white, water-lily flowers, whether there were half a dozen, as in its second year, or two thousand, which is probably the number it produces now.

It's a great privilege to grow something in the garden whose ancestors go back almost 100 million years. Magnolias are one of the first flowering trees; they evolved before bees and were pollinated by beetles. They produce no nectar and when they are at the height of their spring glory it's not unusual to see disappointed bees, attracted by their bright flowers which hold no reward for them.

The tree looks as though it has always been there, its spreading branches now covered in sea-green lichen. All magnolias have thick, thong-like roots, and to keep the plant in good shape where it grows towards the edge of a raised bed, we mulch it annually with rotted muck. Otherwise it gets no attention, apart from us looking at it each time we walk past.

Whatever time of year it may be, these magnolias have something to offer. In autumn both have golden foliage, and before it has fallen next year's flower buds are visible, thickly clothed in pale grey suede. When these cloaks are shed in spring as the flowers begin to open, they carpet the ground underneath. Children love to pick them up and keep them in their pockets – they are as soft as Sylvie.

Life in a Cottage Garden

4

April

April is all about hope. It's the month when everything accelerates. It's a rushing, head-over-heels time; thirty days of rapid, full-on resurgence. It may start reticently, but once it gets going there is no holding it back. Doubts and worries are swept aside with the last of the winter's detritus. It is spring's coronation, when she puts on her crown glittering with the brightest jewels and takes up her throne clothed in a cloak of most vivid green, spreading it far and wide.

There is now a huge urgency to make the garden spick and span lest the brand new, virgin shoots that appear magically, day by day, should have their moment marred by old stems or dishevelled debris. The earth's breaths are deeper and stronger, more urgent now, and nowhere can you hear them more clearly than in the woodland garden. Though there has been activity here since the turn of the year – the entrance of the snowdrops, the advent of the hellebores – April is the time when plant growth expands exponentially. Wood anemones thrust through the leaf mould, finely cut leaves a-quiver, launching their infant buds; buds rapidly become flowers and on the days when

ABOVE AND OPPOSITE
Perhaps more than any other tree (with the possible exception of beech), the Katsura tree, Cercidiphyllum japonicum, *announces the innocence and vulnerability of spring's advent. Its leaves are translucent, new as only spring leaves can be. If there is frost they will shrivel. Please let there be no frost.*

you can feel the sun on the back of your neck, those flowers follow its course across the bright blue sky. Before the canopy fills in overhead (and make no mistake, it will happen soon) there is much to do. These Cinderella plants must push through the ground, open their flowers, attract pollinators, set seed and distribute it, all before the clock strikes twelve – and then sleep once more to wait for another spring.

In the main body of the garden, new shoots and unfurling leaves are the prelude of what is to come; they are an announcement that there is no turning back. In the woodland what happens during April is a one-act play, and by the month's end the main drama will be over.

Some of April's woodlanders carve out a bigger niche for themselves. Trilliums are the aristocracy of the woodland. We have a few clumps of *Trillium chloropetalum* at the entrance to the shady part of the garden. It is a charismatic plant; it has a strangely reptilian air about it, looking slightly mysterious and a little menacing. The three big bracts which it initially sends up are mottled and marbled with maroon, and the three petals that sit on top are deepest crimson. Though so much of the spring woodland is gay and ephemeral, trilliums sound a sinister note.

Gaiety, though, and activity are the order of the day. There are seeds to be sown, seedlings to be pricked out and potted on. The shape and form of the garden begins to emerge. The box hedge is pruned, tulips are carried out and placed – the first splashes of colour amongst the advancing verdancy.

Saturday 3 April

....

Which plant best personifies spring? When I feel optimistic, it is the snowdrop, in a more realistic mood it's the primrose, but in common with most gardeners, I have to say that daffodils are synonymous with spring. Nothing announces its onset so categorically. There may be frosts after its arrival, but by the time the familiar yellow trumpets start to sound, the wheels of the year have begun to grind inexorably forward.

Narcissus pseudonarcissus is our native daffodil. It is small (9 inches high), strong and stocky. The flowers emerge from a papery spathe, gently turning themselves downwards to protect their pollen and to shelter obliging insects inside their deep yellow trumpets. The outer perianth is pale soft yellow. These are Wordsworth's host – the Lent lily.

If I wander out into the field opposite the garden in the early part of April, I am lucky enough to encounter this daffodil face to face. It used to be commonplace in Devon; not so long ago its dancing yellow flowers could be seen displaying themselves in woodland and along river banks up and down the county. Many of its former homes have disappeared, subsumed by development and drainage. To add insult to injury, just as with the snowdrop, unthinking people helped themselves and colonies dwindled or were destroyed.

OPPOSITE *The double jonquil,* Narcissus x odorus *'Plenus' is one of those scrumptious flowers which, once you have grown it, you never want to be without. Because of its thickly packed petals, its yellow is almost orange.*
BELOW *It's easiest to appreciate tiny daffodils in a pot. This dainty variety is* Narcissus bulbocodium Golden Bells Group.

I have tried planting bulbs of *Narcissus pseudonarcissus* without success, but one bulb that does do well at Glebe Cottage is its pale yellow version, *Narcissus* 'W.P. Milner'. This daffodil grows well and is always easy to use. Its soft milky-lemon colouring (just like lemon mousse) fits in with any spring arrangement, and though it is an excellent partner, I also love to plant it on its own, perhaps in tall square pots, where its dainty scale is emphasised and where I can examine each perfect flower.

In my woodland area all the daffodils are white. They are mainly a variety called 'Thalia', a triandrus hybrid. Many of them were planted twenty years or more since but they still flower reliably every spring. They seem to adore the conditions in the damp, leafy soil and light up the dark areas under the trees, pushing spring right down to the big beech hedge.

Over in the brick garden where things hot up in the summer, jonquils seem to do well. Some are planted in big plastic pots lowered into decorative containers (mainly galvanised buckets), but many are planted in the ground amongst aquilegias and euphorbias. Perhaps the most glowing combination is growing alongside *Iris pseudacorus* 'Variegata'. Especiallywhen the broad cream flags of the iris are backlit.

MONDAY 5 APRIL

The Pasque flowers at the edge of my raised beds are in full flower. Both the flowers, stems and petals of *Pulsatilla vulgaris* are covered in down. Before the flowers even think of making an appearance, the finely cut leaves materialise like inquisitive sea anemones. Before they have developed, they are rapidly overtaken by the flowers.

When grown in the poor conditions that suit it best, the silvery sheen is at its most pronounced. This plant relishes thin, alkaline soil (I added lime rubble when I planted mine) and it loves an open, sunny situation. Reginald Farrer, one of the greatest alpine growers of all time, suggests that the Romans carried *P. vulgaris* to England, perhaps unknowingly, by importing seed in lime mortar or stone, and that many of the places where it has naturalised are the sites of former Roman earthworks.

Any plant grown under conditions vastly different from those it is used to in the wild is liable to go through a personality change. The charm of pulsatilla is that its growth is compact and sturdy and very silvery, but a regime of rich soil and overfeeding will make leaves, flowers and seedheads unnaturally tall and weak. It will lose its sparkle. I treat it mean!

The fluffy seedheads that follow the flowers are also disarmingly tactile. Just before they parachute away I take a whole seedhead between finger and thumb and plunge them, tails aloft, into a clay pot of gritty compost. Finished with a layer of grit and watered well, the pot and its contents are then left outside to germinate. I usually leave the pot on the wall next to the mother plant. Since she grows there, so should her seedlings.

Life in a Cottage Garden

THURSDAY 8 APRIL

At this time of year the woodland floor is a patterned place, full of colour and detail. By their very nature the plants who make it their home are archetypal colonisers. The great majority of them live in the first couple of inches of leafy soil created by the trees that form the canopy overhead. At the time when they emerge and flower that canopy is still bare, and they exploit all the available light and rainwater that the tree leaves will steal by the time early summer arrives. I am fascinated by the different methods these plants employ, evolving in a whole variety of ways to make the most of the conditions. Wood anenomes have slender rhizomes; scrape the surface of the soil and you can see them spreading out in every direction, each little branch with its own bud ready to produce flowers and leaves when the time is right.

Anemone x *lesseri* grows in a different way, making dense clumps of rich, green, palmate leaves, beautifully figured in silver and white and scattered with immaculate white flowers from upward-facing buds. These lend even more texture to the picture, and when they are growing in amongst blue pulmonarias with elliptic leaves the pattern becomes richer and more complex.

Pulmonarias of every sort make decorative constituents in woodland tapestries. They love the shade. Many of them have leaves marked with white or silver, sometimes in asymmetric splodges, sometimes margined in silver. Occasionally the whole leaf is silver – both *Pulmonaria longifolia* 'Ankum' and 'Majesté' have sparkling foliage. The leaves of most lungworts are evergreen and continue the show even when their shady associates have gone to ground. They are wonderful with wood anenome *A. nemorosa*, in all its multifarious forms. Our native wood anemone is a charming creature, the back of its sepals soft pinky-grey, the inside pure white. At its heart is a ring of yellow stamens topped by anthers fluffy with pollen. Since it is the indigenous species, this is the one I choose for wild plantings. It is also the most poetic and the one that naturalises best – the more poetry the better! There are places under our enormous *Cornus* 'Norman Hadden' where the double wood anemone, *A. nemorosa* 'Vestal', mingles with self-seeded *Pulmonaria officinalis,* and others where it overlaps with *Chrysosplenium davidianum.*

This delightful little plant brightens up the darkest corners in the shady parts of the garden. It flourishes in damp soil (it is a Chinese cousin of our own native golden saxifrage, which carpets the banks of streams). It has made its home underneath three overgrown alders on the far side of the garden, where its only partners, apart from a few wild geums, are last year's fallen beech and alder leaves. When in its full glory it looks at first sight like a diminutive spurge with bracts around the tiny flowers, lighting up to an almost fluorescent lime green. A couple of weeks ago it was hammered by a hard frost and looked most unhappy, positively dishevelled. I'm thrilled to see today that, magically, it has recovered.

OPPOSITE *Sometimes it is the patterns that plants make that fascinate. Chrysosplenium davidianum is hardly a showy plant yet I visit its site daily when it reaches its peak to indulge in the carpet of green spangled with vivid lime green.* BELOW *Spring combinations abound but most will disband when spring turns to summer and some plants fall asleep until next year.*

OPPOSITE *It's not just my sharpest scissors, but my glasses too that are needed when tackling the removal of the old foliage of* Epimedium x versicolor *'Neosulphureum'.*
BELOW *Removing this old foliage reveals the daintiest of flowers and most tender new leaves imaginable.*

SUNDAY 11 APRIL

As I was driving back from Barnstaple today, crossing the bridge at Umberleigh, I saw my first swallows. I was on my own and though there was nobody to hear me, I couldn't help squealing out loud.

Wherever you live, the arrival of swallows has huge significance. It is a reassurance that summer is on its way and an affirmation that each year follows its pattern. If they are not here by the end of April, we worry that things have gone wrong. But when we see the first pair circling the sky, we know that everything's right with the world.

TUESDAY 13 APRIL

The washing will have to wait, and as for the shopping, not a chance. There's one job I've got to do today that can't wait another moment. One plant that I use all over the shady part of the garden is the epimedium. How can one plant be so useful?

Ostentation is not the epimedium's style. They are modest, quiet plants and even the most boisterous species are no more than mildly showy. Not to say, though, that there is anything bland or utilitarian about them. Although they may be the first port of call when I'm searching for a plant for dry shade, they are things of beauty in their own right. Not only are their flowers fascinating, but the new foliage of both herbaceous and evergreen species has a translucent tenderness that is unmatched by any other genus. Mind you, (and back to the first task in hand) their new leaves can only be enjoyed when the remnants of the old leaves have been removed. This is a job I should have done in February, or March at the latest, but it's mid-April and this is the last opportunity. Already new flowers and leaves are beginning to emerge underneath last year's still presentable foliage. I have to steel myself – taking my sharpest pair of scissors, I trim back the old leaves to their base to allow this year's growth to have its moment of glory.

WEDNESDAY 14 APRIL

Each year I dig up clumps of epimediums, shake off any excess soil and pull them apart, potting them up having trimmed their roots. Last year I made masses and the soil is warm enough now to plant some of them out. The grandiflorum cultivars are herbaceous and are just beginning to show their new shoots. They are the daintiest of the family and I'm planting them where there is little competition, underneath my *Acer* 'Ozakasuki'. Though the ground is full of its fibrous roots, the epimedium will be quite happy – these are plants that thrive in dry shade. In more challenging sites I'm going to use *Epimedium* x *versicolor* 'Neosulphureum'. It's tougher and evergreen, though its flowers are just as refined.

Life in a Cottage Garden

Friday 16 April

Silver-leafed shrubs bring a completely new element to the garden. Many of them have the additional attraction of flowers or catkins. Possibly the foremost example at this time of year is *Salix alba* f. *argentea*, the silver willow. Unlike many of its cousins in the willow clan, its fluffy catkins are borne alongside the first of its fabulously furry silver leaves. With its framework of dark twigs it stands out amongst the emerging greenery of the spring garden, its silver foliage and catkins catching the light.

It is the vanguard of the silver brigade; in a month's time it will be joined by the silver-leafed pear and *Eleagnus* 'Quicksilver' spreading the light into the brick garden.

Monday 19 April

Running through and joining together both sides of the hot bed is an undulating line of variegated box. I grew them all from cuttings and at one time in their infancy they used to accompany me to flower shows held early in the year. I set them free and they have made an ideal evergreen feature in this bed, which reaches its zenith at the beginning of autumn. Without them there would be no interest in the winter here. The soil is rich and plants grow lushly; the box have almost outgrown their place. I'm anxious to keep them but have to find a way to do so in context. Turning them into a formal feature, trimmed and even, would not work, so I've asked Jake Hobson, an expert on cloud pruning, to come and give me his advice. Hopefully he's going to use his expertise to transform my box hedge into a feature that will not only complement the plants in the border, but will also reverberate with the surrounding landscape.

Jake arrives; he's tall enough to tackle a hedge three times the size and makes a beautiful job. He stays well away from one end, though, because a hedge sparrow has built her nest there and one chick has already hatched. When we stand back to admire his handiwork I am thrilled. The form of the hedge echoes the cumulus clouds drifting in the blue sky overhead.

Wednesday 21 April

One of the most magnificent features in the garden for the last few years has been a lone plant of *Eryngium pandanifolium*, a towering South American sea holly. It was planted at the foot of the 'seaside garden' just below my big raised bed. 'Seaside' is a bit of a euphemism; although the bed is in one of the sunniest and best-protected corners of the garden, the soil is heavy clay. In fact, South American sea hollies adore damp sites (they come from the Pampas or, as it's known in Uruguay, the Campos, but they hate winter cold. Mine has died. Out it comes.

OPPOSITE *There are so many touchy-feely plants around at the moment, but* Salix f. argentea *has to be the most accessible. It grows at the edge of one of the woodland beds and already demands that you touch it each time you walk past.*
ABOVE *Touching my poor, departed, South American sea holly,* Eryngium pandanifolium, *its leaf bases soggy and its roots squidgy, fills me with woe.*

THURSDAY 22 APRIL

Fleur is probably a Lakeland terrier but nobody is quite sure. She came to us two years ago by a circuitous yet serendipitous route. She had been abandoned and almost certainly abused. She was a bundle of nerves, never barked and tried to fade into the background as often as she could.

Nowadays she is a different dog. Having puppies has been the making of her, though even their birth was problematic and overlaid with the same sadness that seems to have haunted her first few years. She has a weak heart, a leaky valve, but in the very week we had booked in to consult the vet about the pros and cons of her having pups, she made up her own mind and ran off and mated with a little Lakeland terrier called Ted who lives across the field. Inevitably he's now referred to as Father Ted. When they arrived, two of her four puppies were stillborn, one was so weak he only lasted a few days and the fourth, born half an hour after we thought it was all over, was completely lifeless. Her tongue was blue. For Fleur's sake (she was beside herself and could not even lick the puppy) we refused to accept death, we rubbed the little body, administered the kiss of life and licked her little head vigorously in lieu of Fleur. Eventually there was the tiniest movement in her chest and soon after she began to breathe. She's never looked back – nor has Fleur!

SATURDAY 24 APRIL

A blackbird sits astride the top arched branch of the silver-leaved pear, balancing like an acrobat using the widespread fan of his tail to steady himself as he surveys the scene, assessing what is going on in the brick garden and whether or not anything has changed in the few minutes since his last visit. His plumage is as black as coal, with the same iridescence if you can get close enough to see. You often can; blackbirds are not shy birds, though the cock birds are cockier by far than their quiet brown mates. That blackness and the vivid chrome-yellow beak with the same colour encircling his eyes are there to exhibit his machismo: 'Beware, have respect!'.

When those mellifluous notes issue from his glorious yellow beak, they are assertive: 'Listen up everyone. This is the blackbird calling.' Cock blackbirds may be extrovert but they are the least self-conscious of all garden birds. Noisy too: in their vigorous attempts to unearth food (they are great carnivores and love to stuff their beaks with anything that moves) they turn over debris, leaves, compost et al at a furious rate. Especially when attacking leaves and twigs, their rummaging can be heard from yards away. This handsome chap who bounces up and down on the pyrus is not after worms on this occasion; for the past few days he has been making a bee-line for the ivy tree to feast on its berries and presumably to take some back to his hen, who must be sitting on her eggs close by, probably in the dense undergrowth of our native hedge.

SUNDAY 25 APRIL

One plant that every visitor to the garden seems drawn to at this time of year is the big dark trillium, *Trillium chloropetalum*, which lives just beside the track at the edge of the woodland garden. Everything about trilliums is in threes: leaves, petals, stamens – even the stigma is divided into three parts. They are amongst the most captivating plants in the world, related to lilies yet with a personality quite individual, even esoteric. These trilliums demand my attention each time I walk by.

There is a white form too, with ample flowers, each petal touched with pink at its base. I prefer this one; *Trillium chloropetalum* has a dark, dangerous air, but perhaps that it is precisely why it is so attractive. A North American woodland plant, it seems very at home in the deep woodsy soil laid down by countless autumns of fallen leaves. These plants were originally a gift from my friend Richard Lee, who grew them from seed at Rosemoor. I'd come to know these plants long before he passed them on. He'd shown them to me as tiny seedlings and then every consecutive year since as they grew through infancy, puberty and into adulthood. (Trilliums average seven years to come from seed to flowering.)

Though many woodlanders live in the first couple of inches of leaf mould and colonise readily, trilliums are an exception. They like to stay put and love a deep root run where their strong, white roots can delve into the depths of the humus-rich soil. Clumps build up and may live, growing in stature, year on year in the same site. They increase by seed. Eventually their three-pronged flowers die back, leaving spherical seedheads behind. These swell, covered in a black satin cloak, eventually bursting to reveal pale, thickly clustered seeds. Sometimes the flower stems collapse under their weight and the seeds tumble to the ground. Often they are helped in their journey by slugs and snails, who transport them to nearby sites where they consume what they want, leaving the leftovers behind.

I try to emulate Richard and collect the seed, but often I miss the boat and the snails get in there first. Occasionally, though, they do me a favour. From time to time dense clumps of seedlings appear where seed was abandoned and I can move in, dig them up, pot them on and steal a march. Today I'm digging up a whole group of seedlings, which presumably germinated from one seed pod and have obligingly grown up amongst the gravel on the track. I'm lifting them with a hand fork and, before their roots have a chance to dry out, transferring them individually to small clay pots. Watered thoroughly and kept in a cool, shady place, they should grow on well. These are the sort of plants I really need to keep track of. Next winter they will lose their leaves, though by that time each pot will contain a young tuberous root and next spring a bigger leaf will appear. The process will continue until seven years hence when I may have flowering trilliums to plant out into the garden.

OPPOSITE AND ABOVE
Getting a second chance. Seed I neglected to collect from these handsome Trillium chloropetalum *has germinated and grown. Very conveniently, it has done so at the edge of the gravel track, where I can lift it easily then pot up each seedling. A real bonus.*

When I got up this morning I was determined to put out my big pots of tulips into the places I planned – and I've done most of them. My arms ache. Pot after pot has been carried to various destinations, arranged mainly in rows along paths. Many are already beginning to flower and lend instant splashes of colour to even the bleakest beds and borders.

I plant all my tulips in pots and containers; the soil in the garden at Glebe Cottage is not ideal tulip soil. The wild forebears of our cultivated tulips frequent sunny Middle-Eastern slopes where conditions are poor, dry and hot. Here, they have to face heavy clay, humus-rich and slow-draining, and copious amounts of rain. Although they do reasonably well for one year, they become a dwindling disappointment thereafter and, to add injury to insult, they are prone to the predations of voles, which overnight can reduce a potentially magnificent display to an erratic hotch-potch.

Treating tulips as annuals and growing them in pots has become the practice here. It is extravagant, indulgent and worth every penny. A moveable feast, pots can be centralised through the winter and distributed to key places where they will make the most impact in spring. It's halfway between gardening and flower arranging and there is a sense of control that on this occasion I enjoy. There is also a very nurturing side to growing bulbs in this way – they are constantly under your watchful eye.

I like to experiment with a few varieties I haven't used before (this year I'm trying the Lady tulip, *Tulipa clusiana*), but there are some varieties, trusted and true, that I use year after year. In Alice's garden, on one side, is a magnificent old variety; simple, straightforward and the perfect colour. *Tulipa* 'Jan Reus' is deep, rich crimson and when it is in full flower in a few weeks' time it will pick up the colour of the lovely *Lamium orvala* and contrast with big groups of the pure white *Narcissus* 'Silver Chimes'. On the other side of the pergola, another tulip in the same sort of pots and arrangement but in complete contrast (but not disharmony) to *T.* 'Jan Reus' is *T.* 'Ollioules'. It is pale pink with a paler edge and the colour fades poetically. It has a classic tulip shape, voluptuously rounded and female. I can't help wondering whether or not I chose it for its name, but now that it's out I'm glad it's here. Another tulip I'm using here and in the set of big square pots, which in pairs mark the top of the steps between each of the terraces on the sunny side of the garden, is *Tulipa* 'Purissima'. Aptly named, this is the biggest, whitest tulip you could have. At first its petals have a slight ivory overtone, but as they expand they lose any trace of colour and end up as huge white globes. This is one of the earliest of all the tulips I use. It is flawless. I use its sister *T.* 'Yellow Purissima' in the brick garden, along with *Tulipa* 'Abu Hassan' and *T.* 'Prinses Irene', all glowing hot colours to warm up the place.

Already I'm thinking about next year and making plans for new schemes for April 2011, for another tulip festival.

Thursday 29 April

It's raining today, so I've got an excuse to work in the shed, and there's plenty to do. Throughout February and all through March I have been sowing seeds furiously and some of them are just right for pricking out. One of the greatest excitements this year is *Cosmos* 'Purity', one of the tallest of this race of floriferous summer-flowering annuals, sometimes reaching shoulder height, but at the moment it is tiny. Each plant, barely two inches tall, already has a pair of true leaves and a well-developed root system, and because I sowed them quite thinly they have become robust little plants. I'm giving each one its own individual pot to ensure it can grow on rapidly, ready to be planted out in a few weeks' time. As I gently lower the seedling into its new home, I'm already dreaming about how I shall use my cosmos. Though I want to plant some of them into the borders, they will make unusual subjects in pots – perhaps as replacements for the tulips, many of which are in full flower now.

I grow all manner of plants from seed, from half-hardy annuals to trees. Growing any plant from seed is always thrilling and each time I see the first hint of green on the surface of seed tray or pot, I cannot help marvelling.

Salvias and nicotiana are just two of the other plants I'm growing from seed this year. *Salvia patens* is a spectacular plant with rich royal-blue flowers. It has big seeds, so I've sown each one individually in its own compartment of a module tray. Nicotiana, by contrast, has tiny seeds and they must be sown very thinly on the surface of compost, gently pressed in and covered with grit. In all cases I always water 'from underneath', in other words I stand the tray or pot in shallow water until its top surface (usually covered in grit) becomes damp. When they've drained I carry them off to the greenhouse. It's getting full, and trays of root cuttings occupying precious space need to be moved out to make room. A small seed tray of cosmos soon occupies square yards of space when each seedling has its own pot, and they must be protected until all danger of frost is past.

Friday 30 April

The first rhubarb. Was anything ever so pink? I know it's going to taste delicious. Though one or two plants are forced for this first tender treat, the rest grow on naturally. The first rude crimson buds have started to appear and eventually there will be a forest of stems to pull, stew and enjoy. The bed where it's planted seems very exposed since Marcus Tribe, a brilliant woodsman, visited the garden and laid the hedge. He deftly sliced into the vertical stems at an oblique angle and bent them over until they were almost horizontal, leaving enough wood and bark to ensure that sap could flow from root to shoot. As he worked, he wove the cut stems between stout hazel supports. Gradually the new hedge took shape.

April
Bluebells

OPPOSITE *In the
woodland garden here,
bluebells mingle with
Tellima grandiflora,
geraniums, woodruff and
ferns; all shade-lovers
who prosper in the
same conditions.*
BELOW *Bluebell woods
are part of the national
psyche – nothing could be
more blue.*

Bluebells gladden the heart of even the most miserable
pessimist. Their legions of flowers drift out of sight amongst the trees, on
and on with seemingly no beginning and no end.

They never exist singly or in small groups; we always talk about carpets of
bluebells, for this is how they live. With wild garlic and wood anemones they
must be the archetypal woodland colonisers, spreading exponentially by seed
and spontaneous division, constantly fed with decayed leaves and in total
harmony with their surroundings.

There are ancient bluebell woods where you feel transported to some
mysterious, primeval time. Perhaps the bluebells in some cases have been
there much longer than the trees that now tower above them.

What makes them such significant flowers? Confronted by a bluebell
wood it is impossible not to be in awe of them – there are so many.
Confrontation is the wrong word, though; there is no battle. Instead they
draw you in, you are seduced, mesmerised by an endless mist of blue.

They usually appear just as the first leaves unfold on the trees, pale,
translucent, and as green as green could be. There is enough light for
photosynthesis, their strap-like leaves gorge on the available sunlight. The
swollen bulb just below the surface of the deep leaf litter sends the flower
stem upwards, thrusting towards the light, until eventually the tight, upright
stems with their close-wrapped buds begin to open and extend and the long,
elegant bells tumble from the arching stems.

All across my childhood, pictures of pockets of wild flowers come into
view against a backdrop of coal mines and cotton mills. They were a
testament to nature's supremacy. The furry stems and yellow stars of coltsfoot
breaking through the rubble of bomb sites in freezing Februaries, forests of
rosebay willow-herb, its resplendent pink flowers grander than any garden.
An odd foxglove at the allotment edge, the all-powerful dandelion – wet-the-
beds – pick it at your peril, but the strongest image that comes most readily to
mind are the bluebells.

In Devon nowadays, bluebells start to appear towards the end of April
and into May. When we were children in Manchester, it wasn't until the
beginning of June that we saw our first bluebells. We were lucky to have them.
I used to take my bike up to Oakwood (a misnomer since the prevalent trees
were beech), to inspect their progress, longing for the first true glimmer of
blue. It was a tiny wood lodged between the A6 and the railroad for the local
colliery – still working then, with old carts clanking along the lines, carrying
the coal from the pit to the local depot. The track ran high at the top of the
wood, but at the bottom a little stream meandered, vivid orange from the
iron-ore in the mine workings.

At the first opportunity, as soon as the flowers were truly blue, I would
embark on a picking frenzy. One big bunch of flowers was all I ever took,
I had to ride my bike home one-handed though. They were for my mum and
would always be accompanied by a few twigs of tender beech leaves.

THE BRICK GARDEN

This is the place which most clearly conveys the differences between each season. Month by month the scene changes; grizzled and weather-torn, over winter, by April the debris has been cleared. Amongst green shoots and with the first leaves on the trees, pots full of tulips and daffodils appear. By May's end, camassias take over and after a quiet green summer phase, autumn daisies bring the garden to its climax.

5

May

It's May and celebration is the order of the day. It's froth time in the garden and resistance is futile. It's time to dive in and enjoy!

Everywhere is froth and fullness. It's fulsome and wonderful, it's lush and exuberant, it effervesces. Ditches and hedgerows are thronged with clouds of cow parsley.

Branches of hawthorn and apple are weighed down with masses of blossom, their leaves almost invisible. At Glebe Cottage, apple blossom is one of the most iconic features of May, despite there being only two apple trees and one crab apple. Both the crab and the biggest apple tree are in Annie's garden, one at each end.

It's not just amongst the trees and shrubs in this garden that the frothy festivities continue; it's right down at ground level too. Sweet woodruff carpets one of our shady beds, a little bed on the corner just as you enter the woodland. This is where it all begins; where spring hands over to summer.

Down on my knees planting one of my favourite plants of May, *Ranunculus aconitifolius*, amongst the woodruff, my senses are assailed, overcome by the Mayness of it all. There's the feel of the moist soil between my fingers as it starts to warm

OPPOSITE *Unfurling fern fronds epitomise the sheer energy of May. You are intensely aware of nature's determination to move up and out, and you cannot resist being swept along with it. Woodruff bursts into flower, and (above) apple-blossom explodes.*

Life in a Cottage Garden

up and its earthy smell, redolent of growth and rich in new beginnings, mixes with the scent of the woodruff and the first lily-of-the-valley.

The other half of the garden is only just beginning to waken; initially in May it's the woodland garden that you're drawn to first, and to nowhere more than this bed of sweet woodruff. Smelling of new-mown hay, it's a little plant that was widely used in Elizabethan times as a 'strewing' herb to disguise awful odours. Its scent is light and sweet, but all-pervading too, especially when it is crushed, as it is now by my knees. I'm surrounded by its lovely fragrance. Scent is the most evocative of all the senses, and this perfume carries me back to the very tiny backyard of a house in which we lived in Manchester.

Sweet woodruff has short stems with whorls of bright green leaves all around them, each stem bedecked with tiny little white flowers. Although each flower is minute, when you take the lot all together it creates a glorious foamy impression; en masse the effect is euphoric. Bees and hoverflies move among the white carpet, pausing here and there to gather nectar and pollen.

The hum of busy insects on a warm May afternoon is inspiring. Here in the garden at least, all is right with the world.

SUNDAY 2 MAY

I try to grow salad all year round; of all the vegetables we grow it is leaves that I most love to eat.

Because there was such a cold beginning to the year, I grew lots of salad crops in modules and planted them out when they were big enough and when the weather had begun to warm up. We've had some excellent growing weather, warmth and water, and now beetroot, a cut-and-come-again Italian lettuce mix and several of the Oriental greens (mizuna and various mustards) are ready to pick. Delicious.

TUESDAY 4 MAY

Last year a wonderful thing happened in the garden – well, thousands of wonderful things happened but this was a unique privilege. In the middle of filming in September we noticed a strange new growth on a low branch on the apple tree in Annie's garden, but it was moving! It turned out to be a swarm of bees. Neil, who has been keen to have bees for ages, whacked the branch with a club hammer, catching the swarm in a wine box. He looked after them, but it was late, it was a small swarm, and it was a bitterly cold winter.

They didn't survive. Today, Phil Chandler, the 'barefoot beekeeper', is bringing a top-bar hive and, most excitingly, a new swarm of bees. We are not keeping them for their honey but just for the pleasure of having them in the garden.

OPPOSITE *Suddenly there's so much to keep up with and the vegetable garden is no exception. Amongst all the sowing and planting it's rewarding to be harvesting too.* BELOW *I'm not the only one out foraging, bees are extra busy collecting pollen and nectar. The exotically scented flowers of* Eleagnus *'Quicksilver' are a favourite venue.*

opposite *May would
be quieter but for the
euphorbias which glow
like a series of beacons
through the borders. Both*
Euphorbia palustris
*and the cotinus seem to
have internal sources
of light.*
below *Ricinus belong to
the euphorbia family but
it is their foliage that
provides their spectacle —
but not yet.*

THURSDAY 6 MAY

Our great big euphorbias, the *Euphorbia palustris* in the hot beds, are growing
apace and their huge jumbo heads of concentrated lime green light up the
whole border. In fact, they are a focal point within the entire garden,
complemented by the flickering flame-like leaves of cotinus emerging from
bare branches and back-lit by glorious sunshine. A variegated box hedge runs
through one bed and across to the other side, joining the two together and
giving permanence and structure to the planting. It is clearly visible from
November to April, a real landmark during the winter.

Though the euphorbia is an herbaceous plant, it makes a valuable
contribution to these borders for many months of the year, and during
that time it adopts numerous guises. It is in the spring and early summer
that it is at its most spectacular. All euphorbias have tiny flowers nestling
within bracts or, technically, cyathium leaves. They last for months but
are at their brightest when attracting pollinating insects – which is their
number-one goal. Many have a honeyed scent, too, to make the package
even more irresistible.

Even the shorter euphorbias, *E. polychroma* and *E. amygdaloides*, our native
wood spurge, stand out like torches. They need no staking but *E. palustris*
grows so vigorously in the good soil in these beds that it needs some
assistance to keep it standing. It presents me with one of my most taxing
gardening quandaries; because I love the way it fills in any vacant space in
summer with its rambling stems, a perfect green backdrop for all the fire
I hope to introduce later, it is tempting just to let it do its own thing –
especially when the third act of its drama comes in autumn, when that wealth
of slender leaves turns to glowing gold and its delightful pink stems contrast
so perfectly. But it is a thug and though it is not invasive at the root, its
gangling stems can get out of control. As a first step I'll stake the heavy
flowering stems with stocky hazel twigs left over from Marcus' hedge-laying.
A compromise, but gardening, like life, is full of them.

SATURDAY 8 MAY

Each year I grow *Ricinus communis* from seed. This year I sowed it at the
beginning of February. It germinated well and today I'm transferring the
little plants from their modules and giving each one its own clay pot.
Once they reach this stage they shoot up astronomically. Most sub-tropical
and tropical plants growing in a temperate climate have a huge surge of
growth as the weather hots up. It's still difficult to imagine them becoming,
in a few short months, he-man giants more than six-foot tall with enormous,
crimson, palmate leaves.

The pots go onto the greenhouse staging. We're already short of space but
I manage to squeeze them in.

Life in a Cottage Garden

Monday 10 May

The little pond we made just two years ago looks as though it has always been there. We used to have a bigger pond but I took it out to make way for more paths and walls. I've always felt guilty and wanted to reinstate it. The girls loved it when they were little – frogs, dragonflies and water boatman all frequented it.

Having water in every garden is important. These islands were once a much wetter place – water meadows, ditches and natural wetlands were common. Cleaning out our pond is a major priority if it is to be wildlife friendly; there was a mass of frog spawn this year and the tadpoles have hatched, though they are tiny and thankfully stay at the warmer shallow end, so there is still the opportunity to remove fallen leaves (I should have netted the pond last autumn – it's easy to be wise after the event). All debris is left at the water's edge so any living creatures have a chance to slither back into the pond. There is blanketweed, too, which must be removed if it is not to take over when the sun shines and the weather hots up. Duckweed made an appearance last year, no doubt it came in on some plants friends gave me, but at least its tiny green leaves are easy to spot, though fiddly to get rid of.

The area beyond the pond needs work, too: the soil is heavy here and aquilegias and *Primula sieboldii* seem to relish the damp conditions, so more are being planted. I raised masses of ragged robin last year from seed collected from one plant, and today I'm planting some of them to make a big swathe. The winter has been so wet that new springs have surfaced everywhere and this little patch is now almost a bog garden, so I'll take it as an opportunity to grow a lot of new plants that love to paddle!

Wednesday 12 May

May is one of the last chances you get to plant anything out. It's true that because plants are nowadays grown in containers you can plant out at any time of the year, but if you want to get any sort of 'summer effect' from plants you're putting in, you need to have planted them by the end of May.

In the hot borders there are lots of spaces – well, there are at the moment! Presently there are enormous gaps inbetween, and though I know that the foliage of the euphorbias will fill in and lots of these spaces will be invisible, there's so much else that I want to squeeze in. I'm planting barrowfulls of achilleas and *Rheum* 'Ace of Hearts', geums and more rudbeckias. I'm trying to plant things that are going to take the hot colour on right the way through, but that are hardy and truly perennial. Later on a lot of the colour in this border will depend on half-hardy plants or plants that are downright tender – dahlias and gingers and bananas, cannas and the ricinus grown from seed. I want there to be a feeling of permanence about this bed, as well as an element of theatre.

OPPOSITE *I concentrate on the earth so much it's easy to overlook what an important part water can play. Building this pond was a memorable experience; already it is thriving.*
ABOVE *Planting is my favourite gardening occupation, and if I can divide a few plants in the process, so much the better.*

May 89

Despite the rain, I go out armed with broom and bucket to sweep paths and steps around the brick garden and on the top terrace. The central steps are thick with the flowers of *Cercis siliquastrum*, the Judas tree. When I get there they are far too beautiful to clear away. Sometimes fallen blooms or leaves have a poetry, an eloquence more moving than that of the tree in growth. The Japanese appreciate the fallen leaves of an acer, or cherry blossom scattered on gravel or moss, as much as backlit autumn leaves or flowers of prunus against a blue sky during Hanami, the festival that honours its arrival.

This cercis is a very individual tree; surely every tree, in common with every person, has a unique personality. When it was young I worried that its main trunk leant over, pushed and bullied by the west wind. I thought of staking it and trying to persuade its trunk to grow straight. It was not meant to be. It has been left to its own devices and year by year has adapted itself to its position and to the prevailing conditions. It has settled into its landscape.

My mum grew this tree from a seed pod she picked up from the pavement on a Portuguese holiday. She was delighted when the seeds germinated and when they were big enough she gave me one of the babies she had grown. It has become a significant tree. Each year its bare boughs burst into blossom, the purpley-pink pea flowers emerging directly from the wood. From early in the year its wood starts to show the embryonic form of the flowers that will eventually deck its branches. It is as though the flowers are impatient, unwilling to follow the usual route and emerge from growing tips or laterals; they cannot help but burst out through the bark. Its venerable branches are thickly covered in marine blue-grey lichen, a perfect foil for the magenta of the flowers. It's a wonderful reminder of my lovely mum and how much she loved gardening.

It's getting old now, but when it finally gives up the ghost it will be replaced by one of the young cercis we grew from seed given to me by kind friends. There is so much blossom on the tree this May, it feels as though it is making a special effort, and though it has set few seed pods in the last few years, this year may well be different – a bumper harvest perhaps.

If so, its seeds will be distributed to anyone who wants to try. Growing anything from seed is rewarding, but growing a tree from seed, watching it germinate, potting it on, nurturing it and finally planting it out is magical. If you have enough years to watch it grow into a fully-fledged tree so much the better, but in any case it will be a legacy enjoyed by ensuing generations.

My mum saw her cercis grow here but didn't see it mature, but during its life so many other people have marvelled at its wealth of blossom, enjoyed the shade from its leafy branches and been fascinated by the lichen on its boughs.

I'm glad she picked up the pod from the Portuguese pavement. She loved alliteration too.

MONDAY 17 MAY

Hawthorn, May blossom, provides a frothy icing around the field edges that's obvious from the bedroom windows, making great white cumulus clouds amongst the vivid, fresh green of the other hedge dwellers. When you are up close it is all-enveloping. Today I want to be close to it, feel part of it, not just see it as an abstract vision. There's one wonderful hawthorn, old and immense, that the dogs and I pass on one of our walks. Despite its size, it is dwarfed by an old gnarled oak, which stands behind it as though protecting it – it has its arms around it.

Where I come from we call hawthorn May. It is synonymous with this time of the year. I remember bringing twigs full of its blossom into the house when I was little to let my mum enjoy it too. It is unlucky to bring May into the house, she told me, so we found it a jam-jar of water in the back yard.

Perhaps the superstition has something to do with the fact that hawthorn has two perfumes: in common with other trees in Rosaceae, the rose family, it has a sweetly scented top note with an underlying foetid aroma. Presumably this dual identity has evolved to attract as wide a range of insects as possible, from honey bees to dung flies, to ensure maximum pollination of its copious flowers and thus production of as many of its brilliant red higs or haws as possible. (In Lancashire we call its fruit higs; they were a favourite ammo for my brothers' catapults and freely available.)

The waft of a warm breeze carries the scent of the hawthorn through the garden and turns the emerging beech leaves gently this way and that. Their shadows dance, dappling the ground playfully, the sun shining through them. The leaves are on their way at last. They're soft and translucent and new; these are leaves that have never, ever, been seen before. It is transient, though – in two weeks' time they will have changed, become more opaque, a more solid, darker green. To walk underneath these leaves is a joy to be enjoyed alone, yet one that simultaneously you wish everyone could share.

WEDNESDAY 19 MAY

The garden is full of birds, most of them at their noisiest, building, feeding chicks, embarking on flying lessons and singing still night and morning. There used to be masses of starlings and house sparrows around when we first came here but nowadays they are a treasured sight. The grey of the house sparrow's breast is a perfect match for the grey, newly-emerged leaves of *Pyrus salicifolia*, the willow-leafed pear, and the sparrow's back is perfectly camouflaged amongst the brown of its twigs. This year, appropriately, they are nesting in the eaves of the house. In fact, both hedge sparrow and house sparrow are living up to their names. The little dunnock is nesting in the hedge. She is a much less boisterous creature and even better camouflaged, especially when she hops around on the earth.

OPPOSITE *The dogs love walking in the fields but every so often we stop to take it all in and have a chat. Actually, they look like they're singing.*
BELOW *Hawthorn foliage is often the first out in the spring. With frothy blossom and crimson higs, it is an icon in town and countryside.*

Camas, or Quamash, was an important food source for Native Americans of the North West, who dried it then stockpiled it to help see them through long, cold winters. It is a meadow plant and, unusually for a bulb, luxuriates in damp, rich conditions, loving life here. My camassias are probably Camassia leichtlinii *subsp.* suksdorfii.

Thursday 20 May

No bulb is more at home here than the camassias. From the moment their closely packed flower stems begin to show a glimmer of blue, I cannot resist going out to inspect them every day. It's not so much an inspection as an indulgence.

Though they are wondrous throughout their performance, the lowest flowers on the spike, which open first, begin to look shabby as they are superseded by the next layer. They are at their pristine best as the lowest buds begin to open, the whole flower spike brilliant blue but given an aquamarine or turquoise cast by the green calyces within which each bud nestles. It is only at this stage that the blue of the flowers has any hint of green, otherwise the blue of all camassias is a warm blue, veering towards purple.

In the many new cultivars, this purple or pink predominates. Though some of them have their own individual charm, they are on the wishy-washy side and I prefer the blue of the species. Blue flowers in green grass are always subtly lovely, and because blue is one of green's constituent colours, at long range the two blend together and only separate when we get closer.

Probably the very best venue for camassias is in rough grass – their natural habitat. With good food and an easy life in beds and borders, they can become gangly and flop around like ungainly teenagers overgrowing themselves. Amongst grass they have to assert themselves and seem to thrive on the competition. There is no lawn here at Glebe Cottage, nor even a patch of rough grass, but that does not stop me planting camassias at every opportunity. They are all through the brick garden, wandering around as though they were on their way somewhere. They are in Annie's border still, one of the few plants that stayed in situ when the great exodus followed by the great replanting happened way back in early spring.

Some of the first bulbs I planted have made a little colony now in a semi-shady bed just as you drop down into the woodland garden.

Saturday 22 May

Foxgloves are one of the best May plants. *Digitalis purpurea* and its lovely white form *D. purpurea* 'Alba' are biennials. Frequently they'll sow themselves about but I want their elegant spires every year, so I need to sow them consecutively for at least two years so there will be some plants in flower each May. I'm sowing two different ways, some in a little row at the edge of one of the beds in the vegetable garden and some into half seed trays. It's hot, so I water well.

Seed of white foxgloves is different from that of the purple ones; it's much paler and the whole plant is paler as it develops. It has soft, green, almost furry leaves and there's no hint of purple about its stems, whereas the purple species has darker colouring and purple along its leaf veins, in its stems and right at the base too.

Life in a Cottage Garden

Monday 24 May

OPPOSITE *Two huge plants of* Anthriscus sylvestris *'Ravenswing' sowed themselves in a nursery bed, taking advantage of the fertile soil. They are monumental and their flowers must be admired each time I pass.*

Cow parsley is the essence of May. I never know whether to allow it into my garden, but it seeds here and there and I have to say 'Welcome and thank you'. For fifteen years we exhibited at the Chelsea Flower Show, and as our lorry turned from Pixie Lane at the start of the journey, the ditches and verges effervesced with cow parsley, wave after wave of it rolling along the hedgerows, forcing even dark corners to join in the spumy celebration. Difficult to concentrate on the driving, really!

Standing amongst it on a sunny day, the whole plant is teeming with insects. Although some insects have an umbel of choice, most seem to have catholic tastes and at any one time there may be numerous species of flies, hoverflies and bees, as well as a collection of beetles. Wasps seem to be particularly partial to angelicas, especially *Angelica gigas* with its magnificent platforms of brooding, crimson flowers. Don't be put off, though, wasps do an enormous amount of good, especially when it comes to hoovering up caterpillars – they're always welcome on my cabbages – and hoverfly larvae consume aphis by the hundreds, so Apiaceae are good news all round.

Cow parsley has a host of common names, a sure sign of the fondness in which we hold it. Queen Anne's lace is another popular epithet, and one that perfectly describes the delicacy of the dainty flowers that, in their hundreds, make up each flowerhead.

Few of us have the space to give cow parsley garden room – it has no self-restraint – but its bronze-leaved twin *Anthriscus sylvestris* 'Ravenswing' is welcome in polite society. Its flowers are as attractive as those of the straightforward plant and tinged with pink to boot, but it is its ferny, burnt sienna foliage that tempts you to invite it into the garden.

There are other umbels (now in the family Apiaceae) that embody May's joie de vivre and carry the spirit of the cow parsley's ebullience right into the garden. *Chaerophyllum hirsutum* 'Roseum' is more reserved at first; initially its soft, ferny leaves are almost sessile and its flower stems and buds lie along the surface of the soil, as though too shy to show themselves or looking like some newborn creature. In its own time it lifts itself up and proceeds to branch and fill out, blossoming into a plant waist-high, smothered in myriad tiny purple-pink flowers held in plateau-like heads.

Pimpinella major 'Rosea' has similar flowers; it is a smaller, daintier plant than chaerophyllum, the pink-flowered version of a British native, the greater burnet saxifrage. Its foliage is more succulent than that of cow parsley and the whole plant, though shorter than its hedge-hugging relative, is more erect and compact. Its immensely pretty flowers are a particularly lovely shade of pink with no blue in it, just right for Alice's garden. It provides a warm-up act for the big blowsy poppies like *Papaver orientale* 'Patty's Plum', just starting to bloom at the end of May, then mingles with the rest of the dance floor as June's quickstep kicks off.

Polysticyhum polyblepharum is a corner focal point just as you turn into the wood.
BELOW *The soft shield fern,* Polysticyhum setiferum *'Plumo-Densum' (seen earlier on page 83) has now unfurled, showing off its lacy fronds. Throughout the garden, ferns are making their green presence felt.*

WEDNESDAY 26 MAY

As well as blossom and leaves, there's so much else that's brand new in the garden. The croziers of ferns unfurl so rapidly and have the most magical geometry that you almost feel like sitting there next to them and watching each perfect spiral unwind itself.

This county is famed for its ferns, the damp climate and wooded valleys suit them perfectly. During the Victorian era, fern trains would leave regularly from the North Devon coast for London, their wagons packed with ferns stripped from the north-facing slopes and hedgerows to satisfy the craze that swept the capital. Thankfully, ferns are survivors and there is little evidence now of these former depredations. The high Devon banks positively drip with polypody, one of the most enduring and most useful of evergreen ferns. It spreads slowly outwards, establishing large colonies. On a bank its stoloniferous roots bind the soil together and create pockets where mosses and primroses can make a home. The fronds, about a foot long, are deeply cut and a bright fresh green. Even when it is butchered by mechanical hedge trimmers, its fronds quickly resprout, repairing the bruised and battered hedgerow. It is all through our hedges at Glebe Cottage.

When I need a bold fern with glossy dark green fronds which stands up for itself and achieves a metre in height, I go for *Blechnum chilense*. Although it comes from Chile, under normal circumstances it survives well. Growing in a sheltered corner it has protection from the worst of the weather. It was frozen solid here last winter but has managed to get going again. *Blechnum spicant* is a native plant, half the size of its Chilean cousin but just as beautiful. Sometimes it is adorned with taller, slimmer fronds which bear the spores.

Ferns were really responsible for my settling in Devon. I came in September, to an interview for a teaching job. Perhaps the autumn is not the best time of year to see ferns, but the hedgerows were thick with them and I was completely bewitched. There were all manner of ferns, things I'd never seen before and in such abundance; I just wanted to indulge in it.

Although I've planted quite a few ferns in my garden, most of them have planted themselves. They are the most mysterious of plants. All manner of magical properties have been attributed to ferns, mainly because before the invention of the microscope nobody understood how they reproduced. Folklore had it that spores could bestow the gift of invisibility on those who believed in their magic power.

Just to watch fronds unfurl is magic enough. Somehow ferns embody the power of nature and the way it triumphs. Gardens would disappear without human attention, but most plants would survive, and somehow you feel ferns would be oblivious. Their ancestry stretches back five hundred million years and makes flowering plants look like newcomers who have just tipped up on the botanic scene. They were here long before humans and no doubt will still be going strong long after we cease to exist.

Friday 28 May

The first butterflies are on the wing in May. True, we might have had an occasional visit from a peacock or two, or a small tortoiseshell, in periods of unseasonably warm weather in April (those sort of days when the sun hits your neck and you run inside to rummage through the jumpers and find a T-shirt), but as the first brimstone flutters through the garden there is a sense that this is it. The tide of spring into summer is truly inexorable and nothing can stop it now. Before it was an act of faith, now it is confirmed.

Brimstones are probably my favourite butterflies, they look so like the first fresh beech leaves that emerge at the same time – not only in their pale, watercolour, limey-green, but in their shape, rounded then tapering to a point, and in their texture, veined and only semi-opaque, the bright spring sunlight shining through their wings. I run after them through the garden, unwilling to let them disappear and revelling in the joy of May.

Orange tips, too, are on the wing. Garlic mustard is one of their favoured food plants, so throughout the garden we leave a few self-sown seedlings to develop and flower in the hope of enticing this most dainty and distinctive of butterflies. Adults love nectar from other Brassicacea – honesty, sweet rocket and their ilk are coming in to flower in May. When they emerge, both males and females like to find a convenient perch to dry their wings. The big, fat buds of oriental poppies make a convenient vantage point.

Sunday 30 May

If you are to have level beds in a sloping site like Glebe Cottage, the only option is to make terraces by building walls. The west side of our garden has several terraces, all supported by low dry-stone walls. When we came here there were a few decent stones knocking about in the garden, but they were soon used up on initial building projects – particularly on the walls.

There is such an abundance of leaf and flower above them and living between their cracks and crevices that the walls themselves become a backdrop rather than a feature. Their structure is most clearly visible during the winter, when the whole garden is laid bare, but by May they reveal their true purpose: to offer a vertical home to all manner of plants. The little Mexican daisy, *Erigeron karvinskianus*, one of our most common wall inhabitants, is smothered in its pretty little pink-and-white flowers, but that's not all the wall offers a home to – an extended family of lizards live within it and find the horizontal surfaces it offers the perfect place to bask in the ever-strengthening sun. In shady nooks, fronds of ferns unfurl and wherever they can find a foothold, self-sown geraniums are making a splendid show, accompanied by alchemilla and a host of other plants. With the vertical surface of the wall and the terraced bed it supports, planting space is doubled – one for nature and one for me.

OPPOSITE *A female orange tip,* Anthocharis cardamines, *with perfectly camouflaged wings. The specific epithet refers to one of this species' favoured food sources,* Cardamine pratensis *or, as we used to call it, 'may flower'.*
BELOW Erigeron karvinskianus *makes itself at home between the stones of the raised bed.*

May
Poppies

Just as May changes into June, as I'm lulled into a state of gentle euphoria by the overwhelming froth and prettiness in my garden – suddenly there is a confrontation. A bunch of brilliant beauties burst upon the scene. However fleeting their show, the flamboyant blooms of oriental poppies turn heads and grab the attention of all who see them. They are archetypal shooting stars, bringing excitement to its zenith for a short time, only to disappear at a moment's notice. But that is their raison d'être. The biggest and surely one of the best is the blood red, *Papaver orientale* 'Beauty of Livermere' or *P. orientale* Goliath Group, as it must now be called. Doesn't have quite the same ring to it, does it? This plant is very similar to the wild *Papaver bracteatum*, now called *P. orientale* var. *bracteatum*, a plant of sun-baked Turkish slopes – they must be close relations!

Oriental poppies are some of the first plants to show themselves in early spring. Basal foliage is visible in March. At this stage it makes neat rosettes. It is overtaken by the earliest performers – the pots of tulips arranged along the paths, euphorbias that bring bright splashes of lime green to these borders. Then suddenly without warning the poppy rapidly thrusts up its fat buds wreathed in hairy cases until, one morning, the first case splits and the red, crumpled, papery petals tumble out, unwilling to wait a moment longer, insistent that their time has come. Within hours the bud cases have been abandoned, thrown to the ground or occasionally still hanging on to one petal, before it too, swells to take its place, its puckered surface extending almost visibly, pulled to a smooth, satiny shine. The flower stems are strong and tall, some of them as big as me, and each supports a single magnificent bloom, blood red and boldly imprinted at the base of each petal with a jet-black splodge. The stamens, arranged in a broad circle around the dark, central knob, are topped with an abundance of dark anthers quivering with purple pollen. Poppies produce no nectar but bumble bees in particular love their pollen – it's a giveaway, you know exactly where the bee has been busying itself as it flies around, its broad yellow and black stripes invisible under a waistcoat of purple pollen. As fast as each flowers comes, it disappears. Each lasts a few days at the most and, although one established clump may produce scores of flowers, every individual makes its own statement. There may be a climax with ten or twenty open at one time: some years I miss the main display, coinciding as it does with the Chelsea Flower Show. This year I'm in luck.

I use it in our hot beds, purportedly a mix of flowers and foliage veering towards the hot side of the spectrum – orange, red, warm yellow and lots of bronze foliage to help the whole picture seethe and simmer. The huge, blatant flowers of the poppy get the season off to a flying start.

Elsewhere in the garden other oriental poppies add glamour and, in some cases, intrigue! There are so many exciting oriental poppies which bloom in early summer but none is more voluptuous and dramatic than *Papaver orientale* 'Patty's Plum'. She has to be the true femme fatale of the group.

Life in a Cottage Garden

6

June

Both our daughters were born in June – and me too – so for our family, June is the birthday month. It's a wonderful month to be born, especially if you are lucky enough to be at home and have a garden. As Neil says, 'It's all strawberries and geraniums.'

June is fresh enough to feel new, yet mature enough for us to think of it as fulsome.

When I get home from the Chelsea Flower Show, the garden has changed dramatically – in a week. Everything has clumped up and filled out; there's not a square inch of soil to be seen. Instead of plants surrounded by earth, now all I'm aware of is soft undulations as one plant flows into another.

The garden seems to lose its linearity; you are no longer aware of paths, walls or edges. What takes over your consciousness now is the abundance and generosity of the garden. Where a month ago you could walk the paths deliberately and with a sense of purpose, now you are waylaid, seduced. The garden reaches out and caresses you as you pass. Trees, shrubs, perennials et al join in, racing, rushing and pushing – all falling over themselves to assert the summer.

OPPOSITE *In June flower power takes over. Look how the self-seeded opium poppy picks up the colour of the* Astrantia *'Glebe Cottage Crimson'. So too do the bees on the* Verbascum chaixii *'Cotswold Beauty'.*
ABOVE *Another favourite astrantia, A. major* subsp. involucrata *'Shaggy'.*

Life in a Cottage Garden

The stage is set for the season's flowers, the backdrop perfected. The spring almost seems a rehearsal now, a dummy run for the grown-up stuff of summer. The brilliant colour of our regimented tulips in their clay pots is now a thing of the past and is replaced by an overwhelming greenness. Often in June you can hear the garden exhale, a great green breath pushing out pure joie de vivre. Green holds sway, but not one shade – now more than in any other month I am aware of the predominance of green and of how many nuances there are to that simple word. The beech trees that wrap themselves around one side of the garden are full out but their leaves still have their translucence and newness and are the greenest they will ever be. Walking under them is like being submerged under water.

Everything has burgeoned and expanded. Shrubs are in flower, heavy with scent. Flowers, too, seem to be revving up for a bumper display – bold explosions of colour from flamboyant poppies and peonies and voluptuous cascades of geraniums and roses.

The routine of tying in wayward poppies, beans or sweet peas, dashing in with the twiggy sticks to give them some extra support, reinforces the feeling of growth and reminds us of the cycle where we all play our part. It's very satisfying to help plants do their best.

The summer solstice is an important day in nature and in the life of the garden. Heading for the longest day, there is a feeling of optimism, warmth and a sense of upsurge. Plants, plants and more plants to pot on, feed, mulch and nourish. June is the nurturing month when young plants need attention. An observant eye and an empathetic response now will pay dividends further down the line.

WEDNESDAY 2 JUNE

Alice's garden is a very pretty place. There are roses, masses of softly mounding perennials, and even the two trees within it are 'pretty' trees – a pair of *Cornus controversa* 'Variegata', both of which used to accompany me to flower shows before I planted them for Alice. Although there is no rigid theme, just one glimpse is enough to tell you what she likes. Pink, white and crimson flowers predominate, mingling and merging together in an informal and happy way. Each bed is contained by a straight, broad slate path and on the north side by a wide gravel path. The gravel is pale, almost pinkish, so it lifts the colour within the beds. It's all about levity and sparkle and doesn't take itself too seriously.

It's at its best in June, her birthday month, which is when (with a bit of luck) her rose, *Rosa mundi*, opens its fragrant bicoloured flowers. If Alice comes home for her birthday she can usually pick a bunch. It's an open, sunny site, and the soil is deep and fertile. But it's still clay – and soggy and heavy during the winter – and it's exposed, so everything within it must not only tolerate these conditions but thrive here happily. One genus that does

OPPOSITE *I never thought of myself as much of a pink-and-white sort of a woman, but when I see some of the flower associations in Alice's garden. I'm converted.* BELOW *There are rich crimsons here too. The alizarin pincushions of* Knautia macedonica *nestle amongst the pale, pretty, pink foliage of* Fuchsia magellanica *'Versicolor'.*

particularly well is geranium, and there are some in flower from early May right through the summer. Astrantias, too, would have chosen this as their home, had they had the choice. They don't just grow – they burgeon. One in particular is repeated in all the beds. It is *Astrantia* 'Roma', a sterile hybrid which, because it doesn't set seed, concentrates its energy in flowering non-stop through June, July and into August. Sanguisorbas, with their pink seahorse flowers, *Knautia macedonica* and astilbes in different shades of pink and white add to the picture.

FRIDAY 4 JUNE

As I went just now to make sure the squashes and courgettes I planted a week ago were watered properly, I got quite a surprise. They are planted on a long, raised mound covered with black plastic to keep down weeds and retain moisture, but the plastic started to move, and on lifting it I discovered a big grass snake wrapped round and round and trying to hide itself in a hole in the soil. I wanted to see how big it was, and obligingly it uncoiled itself and slithered away. It was a least a metre long.

SUNDAY 6 JUNE

I'm on my way to plant my leftover French bean plants when I'm stopped in my tracks by a particularly eye-catching plant association. It's not even really of my making. True, I planted *Geranium* 'Brookside' willy-nilly all across the raised beds in front of the house. The idea was to extend the blue and yellow colour scheme within the brick garden up onto the top terrace and right up to the front door. Through one energetic clump in full flower right now, *Eryngium giganteum* has seeded itself. This is the sea holly popularly known as Miss Willmott's ghost. In gardening legend the famous lady gardener, Ellen Willmott, surreptitiously distributed its seed in gardens she considered needed a bit of spark. It is a biennial, but once you have it, it sows itself freely.

The soft blue chalices of the cranesbill look all the more vulnerable in contrast to the silvery spikes of the sea holly bracts. In other places in these beds the same geranium grows alongside, or rather mixed with, a brilliant yellow potentilla, *Potentilla recta* 'Warrenii' var. *sulphurea*, and a completely different picture ensues. Both flowers are the same size and shape and, though their colour is almost opposite, they have similar intensity.

In all effective plant associations the ingredients help each other. The whole is greater than the sum of the parts. Gardening is all about relationships – between the garden and its surroundings, between hard and soft landscaping, and between plant and plant. Putting plants together writes garden sentences, and the sentences tell stories. By using plants whose personae change during the season and by choosing subjects with interesting foliage, flowers and, where possible, seedheads too, schemes can provide

ongoing interest and drama. I incorporate bulbs, too, to supply high points and extra panache. Success depends on choosing the right plants for my soil and situation, and providing that is always the first consideration, it is possible to create all manner of different effects just by the combination of plants. It can be dramatic, deliberately choosing plants whose flower and leaf colours clash – a good clash is worth a hundred insipid associations. In our hot beds I love to use bright red with fierce lime greens (*Euphorbia palustris* does it well), but sometimes I try to achieve a more subtle, peaceful effect, as in Alice's garden.

Colour is not the only consideration, though. There are scale, form and texture too. As if this wasn't difficult enough, the time factor complicates it all. There's no point trying to combine a bright blue delphinium with an orange dahlia if one flowers in June while the other doesn't start until September. But that's what makes putting plants together such fun.

TUESDAY 8 JUNE

Today I'm putting in the first of my summer bedding. Perhaps it's not summer bedding as most people would recognise it. There are no petunias or busy lizzies, but I do use annuals just for the season in pots and containers all around the garden. In two gigantic terracotta egg pots on the front terrace, I'm planting some of the cerinthe plants I've grown from seed, sown way back in the depths of February. Then it was cold and dreary – what a contrast today is. It's bright and sunny and the garden is already full of colour. I remember the first time I saw cerinthe in a garden on the east coast, where the soil was so sandy and well drained that the plants had kept going through the winter and achieved magnificent proportions. Each had made a tall, widely branching plant smothered in glaucous leaves, with strange dark bracts and small, brilliant indigo flowers. Even in my garden, when I look after it and give it sharp drainage and full sun, as in these pots, it will reward me by growing big and strong, and with a bit of luck will flower until October, but it won't survive the winter. Our rainfall level is too high.

WEDNESDAY 9 JUNE

I'm bringing out the pots of cosmos, which are replacing the tulips along the path in Alice's garden, but I don't get very far. I stop in awe to admire *Cornus controversa* 'Variegata'. It's late afternoon by the time I get there and the soft western sunshine is lighting up the whole tree.

This year not only has it doubled in size, but its exquisite green and white leaves are accompanied by plateaux of creamy white flowers. There are hundreds of small bouquets covering the horizontal branches. It is known as the wedding cake tree because of its unique habit. When I planted it, I never imagined it would grow so well or reach such huge proportions. Perhaps if

OPPOSITE *These huge clay pots have seen all sorts of different plants over the years. They have housed agapanthus, tulips, even grasses. Sylvie looks on approvingly as I plant my cerinthe.*
BELOW *These cerinthe were grown from seed sown in March and have made good progress.*

OPPOSITE *What a fine tree this* Cornus controversa *'Variegata' has made, little thanks to me. I used to cart it off to flower shows with its twin. (Which did not fare so well, but thankfully is growing now.)*
BELOW *This year* Cornus *'Norman Hadden' is smothered in showy white bracts suffused with pink as the weather warms up.*

I'd used my imagination, or believed what the books said, I might have been a bit more circumspect about where I planted it. I don't care. It's growing so well, and is obviously so happy, I would rather move the path that passes underneath some of its lower boughs than risk damaging the tree. It's all right for me, I can duck underneath them, but Neil and anybody else of his height or taller really has to go round the other way. As you drive through into the field from Pixie Lane you can see the whole garden across the fields, and this tree stands out like a beacon from late May through until November.

Another very visible tree, though it flaunts itself for a much shorter time, is also a cornus. It was one of the first trees I planted here, though when I put it in you would hardly have called it a tree. When we first came here I used to avail myself of every opportunity to visit other gardens, and Rosemoor was probably my favourite destination. It was then owned and run by Lady Anne Palmer and she had one of the best collections of trees around. In her gardening apprenticeship she was lucky enough to make the acquaintance of 'Cherry' Ingram. Collingwood Ingram had a huge interest in, and knowledge of, all manner of trees, especially flowering cherries. I made a terrible faux pas and imagined from his name that he was a woman. Oh dear. One of the trees which did brilliantly at Rosemoor was *Cornus* 'Norman Hadden', which I met for the first time in late June, adorned with snowy white bracts like enormous four-petalled flowers. The flowers themselves are small and insignificant. The bracts are there to bring in the insects. We gardeners feel they are just there for our benefit. As soon as I saw it, I knew I had to have it. In those days Lady Anne's nursery had very small stocks, but sprawling out of one pot in a dark corner was the one and only *C.* 'Norman Hadden' in the place. It was a self-made layer, which Lady Anne had potted up. Despite its being an unprepossessing specimen, I grabbed it, rushed it home and planted it immediately. For years it struggled, but eventually it took off and it is now one of the most handsome plants in the garden.

FRIDAY 11 JUNE

Once upon a time I was lucky enough to come across a huge copper boiler in a local shop. It seemed no deprivation at all not to eat for the week and bring it home. It has been a major feature of the garden since then. It stands towards the top of the track, and apart from minor adjustments hardly moves from year to year. With a few bricks used as a platform to support large plastic pots, it has played host to everything from troops of tulips to enormous crown imperials, white lilies and ornamental onions. This year the display starts with just such an onion, *Allium schubertii*. Each bulb produces a stout stem and as they burst open they turn into fireworks – maybe a hundred flowers suspended on skinny stems that form open spheres of soft lavender. There is no such thing as an onion with attractive foliage, so I've come out today to remove all the untidy leaves from the base of the stems. Because they are

Life in a Cottage Garden

already shrivelled, my cleaning operation will not be detrimental to the bulbs. In the case of most bulbs the advice is always to leave the foliage intact even after they have finished flowering, so that the bulbs may gather every last ounce of energy from them. Not so in this case. Standing back to admire my handiwork, I'm thrilled to realise the self-seeded alchemilla all around is in full spate. But what's that strange smell? It's onions, of course. I'm going to wash my hands before we eat.

SUNDAY 13 JUNE

I'm off to the greenhouse to check on cuttings. I should have potted on the crambe root cuttings I took way back in the winter. Not only have they made a jungle of deep green leaves so dense the top of the module tray is invisible, but when I try to tug it from the sand bed where it has been sitting I realise that perhaps the roots have gone down as widely as the leaves have gone up. I must pot them on today.

Each one is given a new home in a half-litre pot. The plant from which I took the cuttings is in full flower.

TUESDAY 15 JUNE

I can remember being delighted to discover that little summer cuttings of some of my herbaceous plants would put on roots in a couple of weeks. Normally stem cuttings are the favourite way to increase shrubs and a few evergreen perennials (such as penstemons and some salvias), but this is also a straightforward way of making more of many of my favourite herbaceous perennials.

Today I want to take a couple of trays of cuttings of one of the best asters, *Aster lateriflorus* var. *horizontalis*. Despite having some of the tiniest flowers around, this North American species is one of the most singular of this huge race of Michaelmas daisies. For a start, it has bronze foliage, and though its leaves are diminutive the overall effect is striking. Come September each little branch is smothered in tiny, pale daisies, soft-white with maroon centres that eventually become rusty. The plant never looks dishevelled, and even when the cold winds of winter blow it retains its character. In December, though its stems are wan they sparkle where petals have disappeared, seed has flown and the calyces that remain become polished silver.

Time to stop dreaming. I detach alternate lateral shoots from the stems, holding the main stem firmly with one hand and pulling down gently. Each cutting has a heel, which I will neaten with a sharp knife when I take them back to the shed. I'll strip a few of the basal leaves from each cutting, nip out their tops and plunge them around the edge of pots of gritty compost. Clay pots work the best because not only does excess water drain away, but the clay breathes and new roots receive the air they need.

WEDNESDAY 16 JUNE

I seldom feed my plants, but feeding the soil is almost a preoccupation and it is home-produced compost that I rely on. As I've cleared the garden, leaves, stems and all the detritus have been taken over and piled up next to the compost heaps. Returning from each trip I filled the barrow from one of the heaps built last year, where the contents were rich and dark and ready to enrich the garden.

But it's an ongoing process. I'm ripping out tall stems of chard, which have started to go to seed, and supplementing them with the fresh but fierce stems of nettles growing alongside my native hedge. I'm selective, though, because I must ensure that plenty of leaves remain for butterflies to lay their eggs and subsequently for caterpillars to feast on. The humble nettle is a vital food plant for some of our loveliest butterflies, including small tortoiseshells and peacocks.

THURSDAY 17 JUNE

Well, it's June and the days are long. Having worked all day, it's a treat to wander around the garden and drink it all in – literally, in some cases. Many of June's best scents carry in the air; you're surrounded by them. Sweet rocket, *Hesperis matronalis*, is a cottage-garden favourite, easily grown from seed, and rewards the gardener with glorious nocturnal perfume. It's a commuter's plant, par excellence, pumping out its perfume as the sun drops below the horizon. It is pollinated by moths and, in common with other night-scented delights, has long corolla tubes. Such plants almost always have pale flowers, too, visible at dusk and dawn. It's worth getting up early just to wander through Alice's garden, where the scent of hesperis mingles with the sweet perfume of honeysuckle, Shakespeare's woodbine. If I miss it in the morning, I just have to go out with a glass of wine as the sun goes down.

One shrub in the woodland has delicious scent in midsummer; there are plenty of others with winter perfume but now the scent from this viburnum pervades the air. I wish I could tell you what it's called, but I grew it from a cutting more than twenty years ago and the owner of the garden had no idea what it was. It's massive now, perhaps I should grow lots of cuttings from it and give one to all the people I like. Meanwhile, I'm content to enjoy its perfume, as I'm sure anybody who visits the garden does.

We grow some plants just for their perfume. Dianthus are very pretty little plants, but certainly for me it's their perfume that I enjoy most. *Dianthus* 'Glebe Cottage White' is a plant I first grew from seed collected from a little alpine pink called 'Waithman's Beauty', which had crimson single flowers. It grew up quite unlike its mother. It is neat, free flowering, but above all it has delicious perfume. I propagate as many as I can from cuttings. That's the thing about perfume, you want everybody to share it.

Friday 18 June

There are some plants I could not do without. Top of the indispensible list is *Alchemilla mollis*. Before we came here I had admired alchemilla in every garden I'd seen it in, and when eventually I had a garden of my own, it was one of the first plants I searched for. My enquiries were met with a universal response, 'What do you want that for? It seeds everywhere. We chuck away barrowfuls of the stuff.'

For me that is the attraction. If I were to remove any trace of alchemilla from the garden it would be a different place; all that beautiful soft green foliage, those pleated leaves that catch the rainwater and dew, that froth of lime-green flowers that softens every edge and makes you feel as though you are walking through clouds. If I cut back its spent flowers as they begin to go brown, its chances of seeding are reduced. And if there are too many seedlings I can dig them up and give them to somebody else who is just starting a garden. It is the essence of June, and the lime-green of its flowers is the perfect foil for the soft pinks and blues that pervade the month. It's also a fitting partner for more strident characters, such as *Geranium psilostemon* with its flashy magenta flowers, or the opulent crimson globes of peonies.

Saturday 19 June

Green must be my favourite colour. That is probably because I am a greedy person and there are so many shades and hues of green – certainly within the garden, that they are endless – they'll never run out. Not only do I find the infinite greens within leaves enchanting but I am always on the look out for the frisson of green flowers.

Angelica archangelica frequents road verges close by and though it is a familiar plant it is none the less striking for that, its handsome, architectural form often dominating the scene with its big plateaux of tiny green flowers. Another angelica, *A. pachycarpa*, hails from the Iberian peninsula, although I first came across it in the Bellevue Botanical Garden in Seattle. It stopped me in my tracks. It has umbels of green flowers but its true magnificence rests with its leaves, large and so dark and shiny you feel someone must have been busy with the polish. It is easy to raise from seed, collected fresh from your own plants and sown immediately.

Another unusual umbel with green flowers, this time of the most vivid lime green, is *Smyrnium perfoliatum*. At first sight it could be mistaken for a euphorbia, the bracts surrounding its flowers are such a vivid hue. *Mathiasella bupleuroides* is yet another umbel, this time from Mexico. At first it was kept under wraps, but since it burst on the scene just a few years ago, garden designers and green-flower lovers have sung its praises and used it in their planting schemes. Its foliage looks much like lovage but its flowers are extraordinary, with several branched blooms in each flower head.

SUNDAY 20 JUNE

Most plants have their season and as I walk through the brick garden to sit in the late sun and enjoy the honeysuckle I am aware that this is the meadow cranesbill's time. *Geranium pratense* is an easy, self-seeding plant which can take over in a small place, but here there is plenty of elbow room and I am glad of its ability to fill every vacant spot. It lends such integrity to the garden, as if it had been planted deliberately, though in fact every plant of it is self-seeded. I always leave as many as I can to flower. Although I started with the native blue form – just one plant from a wildflower nursery, there are now plants with pale grey, lavender and even lilac flowers – the whole range. They soften edges and disguise bare spaces. There are big clumps now amongst self-seeded fennel, their pale blue chalices showing up beautifully amongst the fine, ferny filigree of the fennel.

As soon as their petals fall I try to cut them back to make room for summer flowers that will give a longer show, but very often they are in flower again within a month. In fact *Geranium pratense* is so at home in my garden, self-seeding prolifically, that unless I am assiduous about decapitation and equally brutal about taking out unwanted youngsters who have already established a foothold, we are overrun with meadow cranesbill. But some summers, when I have missed my mission in the previous year, I am glad I did. The garden is a sea of colour, from white and palest grey, through pale lilac to every imaginable shade of blue. *Geranium pratense* is covered in fine down but you are unaware of this until you see it backlit by the evening sun.

There are two double varieties of *Geranium pratense* which pose no threat of invasion. As with most double flowers, they have no ovaries and are incapable of producing seed – sad for them, but fine for gardeners. Once most plants have been pollinated they have no further use for their petals so they just fall away, but in the case of many double flowers pollination cannot occur and the flowers last much longer. *Geranium pratense* 'Plenum Caeruleum' starts in early summer, sending out stem after branching stem of warm blue flowers verging on lilac and carrying on its long display until the autumn. It is just as devil-may-care in effect as many of its single siblings, but for obvious reasons never develops their typical 'cranesbill' seed heads. Its flowers are loosely double, whereas the flowers of *G. pratense* 'Plenum Violaceum' make symmetrical rosettes. Each flower forms a separate posy and each stem produces great bunches of flowers, until the plant looks like one enormous bouquet. The shape of each flower is completely formal.

The soft colours blend so easily with nearby plants there are never problems with neighbours. As well as enjoying its clouds of bloom, each individual flower is a delight. The rounded petals overlap one another and where they do the colour is doubled in an ellipse, and the anthers and stamens make a further neat pattern. On the reverse the calyx forms a green star.

MONDAY 21 JUNE (SUMMER SOLSTICE)

For me, the Summer Solstice is the most magical day of the year. The day the year reaches its height; when you feel surrounded by the summer and as far away from the depths of winter as it's possible to be. The weather is warm and sunny today – just as it should be.

WEDNESDAY 23 JUNE

Although the track between the shady and sunny sides of the garden used to be broad, it has shrunk. Islands of self-seeded plants make little gardens amongst the gravel and, providing everybody can walk through, they ensure a pleasant meandering way up to the house and an introduction to the gardens on either side. Sometimes, though, there are so many self-sown seedlings on the side paths that meet the main track, it is difficult to distinguish beds from path. This morning I've filled a big wooden trug full of small pots of compost and I'm lifting some surplus seedlings of *Geranium nodosum*. This is a prolific geranium, excellent in shady conditions. It flowers all summer long, has evergeen foliage, yet still takes autumn colour.

I have a very special form, called *G.nodosum* 'Dark Heart', whose centre is deep purple. Each seedling is nestled into a separate pot. I'll water them well, stand them in a shady place, and when they've established a good root system, put them back into the garden.

THURSDAY 24 JUNE

Today is my birthday, my 65th one, and it's a beautiful sunny day. A couple of days ago, when I was away filming, Neil brought my birthday present into the garden. Although it's too big to miss, I've been steered past it and not allowed to inspect it until today. It's a magical Romany caravan, totally authentic and hand-painted by one of the few remaining exponents of the art. Now Neil leads me by the hand, pulls down the steps and I'm invited to open the doors of my new home from home. It's almost as beautiful inside as out. It's carpeted throughout, including the ceiling. There's a proper little wood-burning stove, too, and lace curtains. Now, where's my crystal ball? I can feel a new career coming on. It's parked up next to the pond, facing in the right direction so that when I get the piebald pony (my next birthday?) I'll be able to head straight off into the sunset.

June is birthday month at Glebe Cottage. Both Annie and Alice were born in June – Alice on the 15th and Annie on the 29th. Neil's not too left out, though, his birthday is the 22nd July. So June is a month of celebration, not only for us but in nature too. Every morning is bright with birdsong and the garden is full of undulating growth and frothy flowers; as you walk about you can feel the plants embracing you.

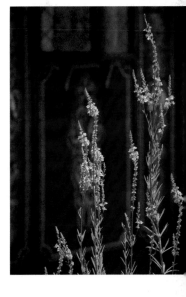

OPPOSITE *I'm so happy. I don't want to go anywhere or do anything, just sit here and let everything flood in. Later Neil will make us food – some of it picked from the garden. We can sit out late.*
BELOW Linaria purpurea, *purple toadflax, has self-seeded behind the caravan.*

June
Roses

There aren't as many roses as there used to be in the garden at Glebe Cottage. I planted several old shrub roses, including *alba*, *centifolia* and moss roses, close to the cottage when Annie, our eldest daughter, was a baby. They arrived as a bundle of bare roots in the winter and, having no previous experience of such things, I felt they were doomed to failure. By the time Alice, our youngest, arrived (there are just less than two years between them) the roses were thriving and blooming. The former rose bed is now a vegetable garden, but some of its previous occupants inhabit new venues in other parts of the garden.

We always try to cut a few roses for our birthdays; Alice's second name is Rosamund, so *Rosa* 'Rosa Mundi', with its strikingly striped flowers of pink and white, lives in her garden. So too do *Rosa* 'Little White Pet' and *Rosa* 'The Fairy', with its multitudes of small pink flowers, which combine well with astrantias, *Lamium orvala* and green-and-white hostas. All these roses have excellent scent but the rose in our eldest daughter Annie's garden has even better perfume. *Rosa* 'William Lobb' is a lovely old moss rose with a deep, luscious fragrance. If you rub the 'mossy' buds they also exude a sweet aroma. The first flowers of this rose are lavish, richly petalled and full to bursting with colour and scent – the best reasons to grow any rose.

June is all about fragrance and roses have it in abundance, including many of the climbers. Growing into the now huge *Cornus* 'Norman Hadden' and spanning the track to climb into the branches of the crab apple, one of the best of all these riotous climbers, *Rosa* 'Paul's Himalayan Musk' fills the air with scent. As with many of these climbers, the show is short but while it is at its peak there is nothing in the garden to touch it. The flowers are small but full, borne in great bunches; the foliage has a glaucous cast, a perfect complement to the pink petals.

We have a more modest climber, *Rosa* 'Sander's White', growing over an arch with a honeysuckle, *Lonicera periclymenum* 'Belgica' the 'Early Dutch Honeysuckle', in Alice's garden. The rose has fresh dark green leaves and it produces its perfect double white flowers for several months during the summer. It has a pleasant appley aroma very similar to that of *Rosa* 'New Dawn'. This is perhaps my favourite rose, with its neat buds the colour of pink flesh opening to the palest creamy pink. I remember 'New Dawn' climbing along the black fence in our little garden close to Manchester, Nobody had painted the fence, it was black from factory smoke, but the sulphur in the air kept rose disease at bay and there was never blackspot on the leaves. Come to that, both *Rosa* 'Sander's White' and *Rosa* 'New Dawn' are resistant to most rose pests and diseases.

In Devon we have clean air and rose complaints are much more prevalent, but neither of these varieties seems prone to attack. I garden organically so roses have to be able to fend for themselves. I try to grow them as their forebears grow in nature, surrounded by grasses, perennial flowers and sweet herbs.

Life in a Cottage Garden

ALICE'S GARDEN

*In the cold days of winter and early spring, Alice's garden seems
a barren place. By summer it is a scene of fecundity, and though
it reaches its peak in June, its flowering continues through to the
frosts. In spring it is a sea of undulating clumps of perennials lit
with pots of tulips, by July the white phlox that Jeannie, my
mum, gave us makes big pale splashes that are especially lovely
in the evening.*

7

July

Rain at last, burgeoning, wild, and on the edge. There is a heart-in-your-mouth feeling of insecurity as the month of July begins; it would be like juggling, except whether or not all the balls stay up in the air seems a matter of chance rather than one of skill. More often than at any other time of the year, you realise what a large part luck plays in the success of your plans and in the well-being of your garden.

It's been very dry, the driest year for 80 years. The lanes and road verges, not to mention the poor fields scraped of their grass, are looking tired. The edges of the garden, too, were beginning to look the worse for wear. Astrantias were hanging their heads, moss was losing its verdancy and was on the cusp of becoming crisp. But all that has changed, for now at least. I realise I keep talking about how unpredictable the weather is here and that is the point: because our weather comes from the Atlantic it can change so rapidly it is almost frightening. Well, more exciting than frightening. July can manufacture storms, limpid days of full-on heat and wall-to-wall sunshine where nothing seems to move, or skies where cloud dashes at breakneck speed, so

OPPOSITE *Comma butterflies are special somehow. Perhaps it's just the edge of their wings, seemingly cut out with pinking shears before the butterfly was given life. Here a slightly bashed and bruised comma gathers succour from the sweet nectar of veronicastrum.*
ABOVE *A female broad-bodied chaser dragonfly takes in the July sun.*

Life in a Cottage Garden

rapidly it's more mind-blowing than the effect of some psychedelic drug.
I can remember when we first came here, having been used to snatches of city
sky glimpsed occasionally between rooftops or from the top deck of a bus,
standing in the middle of the garden (little more than a field then),
bewitched by the sky and turning a full 360 degrees to take it all in until
I got dizzy.

In total contrast to those whizzing skies, there are languorous days in July
when the air is still and heavy, when no breath of wind stirs, when you can
hear the crackling of dragonflies' wings as they chase across the garden. The
air is abuzz with insects, all on a mission. Only the butterfly's flittering flight
seems random as it moves from flower to flower, drinking deeply from the
nectar within.

TUESDAY 6 JULY

The seeds of *Omphalodes linifolia* are already set and some are ripe enough to
collect. This has to be one of the prettiest annuals around, and although it
will self-seed in an arid place, the garden at Glebe Cottage is anything but
that. I collect the seed each year in several instalments, store it in paper bags
and then, in early spring, sow individual seeds in module trays. The seed
hardly looks like seed at all: it is papery thin and its middle seems to be
missing. Its easy to see why this plant is also called navelwort – both flower
and seed have little dimpled centres. With silvery leaves and low clouds of
tiny white flowers, it pretties up the raised bed and the seaside garden like
foam gently spilling over the edges.

THURSDAY 8 JULY

For sheer glamour and intoxicating perfume, lilies are unparalleled. I rely on
them to add pzazz and step things up a gear where areas of the garden have
slowed down in July. There is one clump of lilies in the hot garden that leads
the way. I bought it as a growing plant rather than as dry bulbs and have
never known its name. In the rich, much-improved soil in one of the hot
beds, it has made itself very much at home, increasing year on year. But is it
the right colour? Perhaps it has too much crimson and not enough red?
When I decided to move it, lifting a heap of bulbs, potting them and
increasing them, my efforts were half-hearted – perhaps I wasn't really
convinced it should go. I must have missed some bulbs. Instead of it
disappearing it has increased with strong yard-high stems, each well-
endowed with up to ten magnificent trumpets. One of the reasons for
wanting to move it was its proximity to two big clumps of a handsome day-
lily, *Hemerocallis* 'Stafford', whose flower colour perfectly fits the job
description for the hot beds, burnt orange, baked earth, Grand Canyon
colours. Didn't they clash? Did something have to give? But when the gap in

OPPOSITE *What a
jubilant lily this is. It just
carries on — healthy,
happy and completely
oblivious, untrammelled
by my efforts to move it.*
BELOW *Seed is ripening
all around the garden
and I must make every
effort to catch it. You
don't come by the seed
of* Omphalodes
linifolia *in many
catalogues; I prefer to
save my own.*

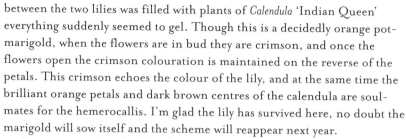

between the two lilies was filled with plants of *Calendula* 'Indian Queen' everything suddenly seemed to gel. Though this is a decidedly orange pot-marigold, when the flowers are in bud they are crimson, and once the flowers open the crimson colouration is maintained on the reverse of the petals. This crimson echoes the colour of the lily, and at the same time the brilliant orange petals and dark brown centres of the calendula are soul-mates for the hemerocallis. I'm glad the lily has survived here, no doubt the marigold will sow itself and the scheme will reappear next year.

I am not a one for deadheading, at least there seems to be little time for it; it would be lovely to find time to do it and it makes an enormous difference to the performance of plants, but when it comes to day lilies I have to make an exception and practise what I preach. Flowers of day lilies seldom last more than a day – that's how they got their name – but if old flowers are removed religiously as they fade, the whole plant continues to look new, fresh and vital. It is a satisfying job to twizzle the dead flowers from the plant and there is no regret; they have had their moment in the spotlight, as gorgeous as could be, but now they must stand down and allow others to take their turn.

Some people develop a thing for day lilies. Devotees abound and each year scores of new cultivars are introduced, many of them incredibly showy. In the garden here their numbers are limited. Most are yellow, close to the species. My hands-down favourite is *Hemerocallis lilioasphodelus*, a charming species and one of the first to flower. Its perfume is sweet and pure. This is one daylily I never deadhead since it sets seed easily and the spherical seedheads are one of its most charming features. You can eat the flowers, too, they look exquisite in a green salad, taste fresh and have a crunchy texture. This day-lily can be increased by seed, or by division. The latter job is an easy but energetic occupation.

Early or late in the year, in March or November, great clods of day lilies are hauled from the earth and given the twin forks treatment. Back-to-back garden forks are plunged into the centre of the clumps and used as a lever to pull them apart. When they are small enough and any old centres have been removed, pieces are replanted.

Sunday 11 July

When it comes to true lilies, though, I use a different method which relies more on dexterity than brute strength. When new lilies arrive in the spring, or when I am moving their bulbs around in the garden, I can never resist taking a few scales to make new bulbs. Separate scales must be detached cleanly at the base of the bulb and mixed with slightly damp vermiculite. I shake the bag regularly as I'm lowering the scales into the vermiculite, tie it up, put it into a pot and cover it with grit to exclude light. Thinking about lilies the other day reminded me to go and check on the lily scales.

MONDAY 12 JULY

I love reptiles and the thought that they frequent my garden is thrilling. To find slow worms, snakes and lizards whilst working amongst my plants is a privilege and I know that it would happen far less frequently, if at all, if I did not garden organically. Organic gardening is perhaps the most hotly debated topic amongst gardeners. Anybody would think it was a new idea.

The irony is that, far from being revolutionary, we human beings have grown our gardens and cultivated our vegetables organically since we started to produce our own food. It was the chemical revolution, the widespread use of fertilisers, pesticides, herbicides and fungicides that was parvenu, alien, the new-fangled upstart.

Growing organically is a system; it cannot be partial, it has to be all or nothing. It is a way of creating and maintaining a sustainable scheme that follows and emulates nature, because, especially when growing food, we are asking more of the soil than Mother Nature would – so we help it to work by adding more of the same constituents it produces itself. We can make compost and leaf-mould, we can use rainwater and natural liquid feed and encourage beneficial insects into the garden to help deal with pests. In turn bigger creatures, like my slow worm, become part of the system, able to find shelter and food. These methods promote strong and healthy growth and enable us to grow intensively without upsetting the natural balance.

Chemical gardeners use fertilisers to boost plant growth, they see the soil as somewhere the plant grows, somewhere that holds the fertiliser with which they are 'feeding' the plant. However, prolonged use of chemicals results in the death of micro-organisms and eventually the soil becomes a barren place.

As an organic gardener I know that the soil sustains life and the natural process by which nature recycles material – to feed the soil, to produce plant growth, to provide the material for recycling – is an ongoing process. It has worked for millions of years in nature and for thousands of years when adopted by us in our gardens. As an organic gardener I feed the soil and the soil feeds the plants.

WEDNESDAY 14 JULY

This year I've grown all our tomatoes in the greenhouse. Last year potato blight was such a problem it wiped out both our potatoes and tomatoes. I was not alone. Up and down the country people's crops of these two favourite vegetables were decimated. This year we're growing our spuds in containers and our tomatoes under cover. In their native habitat the antecedents of our cultivated tomato varieties make enormous scrambling plants. I've made our plants a scaffolding tunnel with bamboos so they can grow as freely as possible, with the maximum amount of light and air. This means they must be tied in regularly, especially now that the fruit has started to set.

ABOVE When staking tomatoes I always tie the string onto the cane first. OPPOSITE Slow worms are legless lizards but move in just the same way as snakes. It's hard to resist picking them up; their skin glistens gold and bronze. Sometimes I find groups of them around the garden.

Some tasks in the garden are very seasonal, specific to a particular time of year, but there are others which may not seem so crucial that need to done over long periods of time. Deadheading belongs to the latter category, but because there is no imperative – nothing will die if it is not done – I often neglect it.

Yet it is one of the most satisfying jobs in a garden and one of the few jobs where you can see an instant improvement. Not only do plants look much smarter when they've had their dead and dying flowers removed, but I know that when I do find time, the further flowering of the plant in question will be much improved and almost certainly much prolonged.

Cosmos 'Purity' is splashed throughout the garden this year. I've used it in pots and planted it directly into the ground right through Annie and Alice's borders and in the bed below. It lends cohesion to this part of the garden, though I would not want to put it anywhere near the hot beds or the brick garden. Some gardeners think that adding a dash of white is a good way to avoid colour clashes. It's a cowardly way out. Better to use white for itself. It isn't always easy; white reflects light and is difficult to concentrate on in bright sunshine. Although the cosmos has showy flowers, they are held on branching stems and mixed with fine, fuzzy foliage, which helps them have a light, lilting look rather than creating a sheet of white.

Some gardeners use secateurs for deadheading, but I always use scissors or some little Japanese fruit pruners. Accuracy is needed, especially in a case like the cosmos. There are often several flowers in close proximity, some of which may be just coming out whilst others have had it, and I don't want to make any mistakes. Each flower and its supporting stem is trimmed back cleanly to the main stem from which it emerged. With judicious deadheading, these plants should produce flowers right through to the first frosts, but I must remember to keep on top of it and to regularly deadhead all the other annual daisies I'm growing.

Not all plants need such finesse when it comes to cutting back. Many herbaceous plants produce only one flower or a spike of flowers on each main stem; *Cirsium rivulare* 'Atropurpureum', a handsome crimson thistle, makes a little clutch of flowers at the top of each stem. Eventually they change to thistledown, but there is no seed amongst it, so it is not worth keeping. At the first sign of disintegration I move in with the pruners and cut the stem back to the ground. It would be pointless to take away individual flowers. The same is true of many campanulas: better to allow all the flowers to open then fade before cutting down the stem, but when that has happened to cut it down completely. There are some flowers, though, which I don't deadhead. Many plants are prized as much for their seedheads as for their flowers. Often this is an aesthetic consideration, but sometimes it is because I want to save the seed or leave it for the birds to enjoy.

Friday 16 July

Planting out continues in the hot beds. Already there are vivid flowers; *Lobelia tupa*, far from succumbing in the big freeze of January and February, has made spectacular progress and its tall spikey stems are decorated with their strange red flowers. I'm adding another quite different lobelia to the bed. It's *Lobelia* 'Queen Victoria', a familiar, though still exciting, plant with dark beetrooty leaves and dense spikes of searing red flowers. I'm dividing each plant into three as I put them in and they are still decent chunks with several basal rosettes and a couple of flower spikes apiece. They immediately strike a chord with the castor oil plants which have now made themselves completely at home in this sun-baked corner.

Sunday 18 July

Opinions vary hugely amongst gardeners as to the rights and wrongs of using tropical and subtropical plants in the environs of an English garden, especially in a cottage garden such as mine. One school of thought is that nothing should deviate from the ideal of pastel colours and pretty flowers. On the other hand, pioneering gardeners like the late Christopher Lloyd feel that rules are there to be broken; a sense of fun and adventure informed everything he did. When he ripped out the tired old rose garden at Great Dixter and replaced it with his 'Tropical Garden' it was done in a spirit of enterprise and with his usual panache. Every year he tried new experiments, both with individual plants and with the way in which he combined them. He understood his plants and their requirements so well and was always prepared to learn from his mistakes. Both the man and his writing were truly inspirational; Fergus Garrett continues in the same vein today. Many of the plants that I use in this hot border I met for the first time at Dixter.

Gardeners share the same vocabulary; we use the same plants but each of us uses them in our own way. Gardening is one of the few ways by which we can express our individuality and is the most direct route we have to connect us with the earth.

Monday 19 July

My garden is full of slugs and snails. They're an important part of the food chain. Hedgehogs, thrushes and blackbirds feed on them and they keep down the debris and detritus that the garden produces. This sounds very altruistic, but of course there are some times when I curse their munching. The lobelia that I planted just a few days ago have been decimated by the predations of gastropods. Not much I could have done about it except to plant something less to their liking. I've added some *Rudbeckia* 'Rustic Dwarfs' to this planting and they are unscathed. They have hairy leaves and stems.

OPPOSITE *Little did I realise when carefully planting lovely new divisions of* Lobelia *'Queen Victoria', that only days later they would be ravaged by slugs and snails* BELOW *The evidence. Experience should have taught me that these juicy stems would have been irresistible.* Lobelia tupa *was untouched.*

One of summer's treats is 'taking out the dahlias'. It sounds like some ancient ceremony but I've only been doing it for a few years. Doubtless there are thousands of others too who practise the same ritual, but perhaps not in quite the same way. Many gardeners lift their dahlia tubers each autumn, after the foliage has been blackened by frost, and store them in old compost or bark over winter, potting them up in spring, watering and feeding them, then planting them out again when all danger of frost is past. My routine is lazier – plants are kept in their pots, underneath the greenhouse bench, and water is withdrawn. Only when spring comes again are they topped up or potted on and brought back to life.

Rather than planting them, I 'stage' them, arranging their pots either on the ground or on top of upturned pots in strategic positions through the hot borders, where they spend the summer surrounded by other sub-tropical exotics – ornamental gingers, ricinus and cannas. The dahlias are heavy enough, but some of the hedychiums have been grown in pots and I can only just lift them. It pays to decide exactly where I want them to go before I lower them into place. Next year, when they will be so much heavier, I am going to need a hand. Either that or take up weight lifting meanwhile.

There are hardy shrubs here – bronze-leaved *Cotinus coggygria*, purple elder, and the cloud-pruned variegated box hedge which forms the central spine of these twin beds and a background to the flowers of red, yellow and orange that will predominate throughout the border. Yellow rudbeckias, russet-orange, brilliant red and amber crocosmias will take over later, but the dahlias have started to flower already: pillar-box red 'Bishop of Llandaff', 'David Howard' in pale orange and dainty 'Ragged Robin' with skinny, slender, dark-red petals. There will be some new recruits this season, a dozen or so plants grown from a seed strain called 'Bishop's Children'. They have made promising plants from an early sowing, all with dark leaves. I can't wait to see the colour of the flowers!

FRIDAY 23 JULY

When they were little, our daughters Annie and Alice were always protesting about where we lived – in the middle of a field. They are both keen on the sea and could not understand why, since we had to live in Devon, we did not live within sight of the waves. I love the seaside too and one of my favourite excursions is to Braunton Burrows, a unique and strangely beautiful area of sand dunes forming an almost lunar landscape alongside a huge stretch of elemental sand and sea. Though it is used occasionally for grazing and by the army, it is essentially a wild place, its flora and fauna in total control. It is one of a limited number of places around our shores where the true sea holly, *Eryngium maritimum*, abounds.

SATURDAY 24 JULY

Walking round my garden I'm struck by the number of different situations that exist within its limited confines. It's less than an acre, yet there are places where I can grow woodlanders, others where high alpines will thrive and yet others that have the feel of a meadow or even the prairie. This allows me to grow a huge range of different plants. On the sheltered shady side, I can grow plants from Chinese forests or English woods. Epimediums from Asia, Europe and America, and wood anemones, natives of our own deciduous woodland – all these are plants that are going to thrive amongst the roots of the trees I've planted. Pulmonarias, trilliums and erythroniums prefer a richer living but still love shade. I enrich the soil with old compost and leaf mould to ensure that they grow well.

In the opposite situation, in full, glaring sunlight and impoverished soil on my raised beds and in the 'seaside' garden, the plants that excel come from seashores or Mediterranean slopes – everything from sea-hollies, like *Eryngium bourgatii* and sea-kale, *Crambe maritima,* to lavender, cistus and rosemary. All would resent extra nourishment. I never mollycoddle them. Should I feed them with rich organic matter, they would grow like fury then turn up their toes and die. The regime that holds sway in their natural habitats is one they must have in their new home here.

And if plants are to face exposure not just to high winds but also to cold and wintry blasts, then the vegetation of moor and mountain signposts the way to go. Pulsatillas and phlomis are perfectly at home on the edge of my raised bed, joined by the little Mexican daisy *Erigeron karvinskianus.*

Coming down from the mountains and into the wet and boggy ground around my pond, the plants I choose are those that have adapted themselves to paddling, floating or swimming underwater. There is such a wealth of wetland plants to choose from. Many are native, *Iris pseudacorus,* ragged robin and *Butomus umbellatus.* There are a few exotics too, Japanse irises and a rodgersia or two.

The garden at Glebe Cottage is long and narrow and bounded on all sides by hedges. The plants that thrive here need to be versatile and adaptable. They must withstand sun and shade, damp and drought and often share soil with hungry hedges and climbers. The plants that inhabit our native hedges and ditches have long had to fend for themselves – foxgloves, meadowsweet, eupatorium and Solomon's seal. Whether they are species or cultivars, it is these plants that thrive around the inhospitable boundaries. In the open garden, plants of meadow and grassland are completely at home. They form the mainstay of my beds and borders; stalwart plants not averse to mixing and mingling with neighbours and capable of putting up with a wide range of conditions. Their family names are so familiar: bellflowers and cranesbills, daisies and poppies. And all I have to do is choose the right plant for the right place. What a treat.

OPPOSITE *Astilbes and astrantias could have chosen this spot in Alice's garden for themselves. The soil is rich, fertile and never dries out. Ideal.*
BELOW *This hilarious 'walking onion' has adopted this bed as its home, although it has already roamed to the other side of the track.*

SUNDAY 25 JULY

Once you have saved your own seed and sown it, pricked out the seedlings, brought them on and planted them out, gardening takes on a different meaning. I love saving seed, it's central to the way I garden.

The garden is always fecund at this time and this year it is exceptionally so, because so far we've had a real summer with extensive hot, sunny spells last month – flowers have produced more bloom and yielded enormous crops of seeds. Perhaps it is most exciting collecting seed from herbaceous perennials, simply because it's the most obvious way to propagate them. If you divide a plant you may make several new clumps, but if you grow from seed there will be enough to satisfy even the greediest gardener and plenty to swap, too. In every case, observing nature and emulating what she does is the most successful game-plan. Perennials have different ways of distributing their seed, but if you can catch it just at the point when it would fall, fly, or explode, it is bound to be ripe and ready. Often this is when capsules begin to dry and turn brown. Sometimes aquilegias seem to think the garden is there just for them and their procreation. They seed themselves effusively with gay abandon. I could just leave them to their own devices, but occasionally it's nice to feel you can put some of them where you want them rather than just where they want to be.

They are amongst the earliest perennials to set seed. On the raised bed some may already have fallen, but other seed pods are still standing erect, rattling whenever they are touched or the wind blows briskly.

I capture them by carefully slipping a paper bag over the whole collection of heads, grasping it tightly and severing the stems with scissors. I invert the whole caboodle, tying the neck of the bag with twine, and I take it over to the shed, hanging it out of direct sun but where the air can circulate around it.

It's fascinating to carefully examine seed heads and discover just how their seeds are dispersed. Hardy geraniums and euphorbias, for example, catapult their seeds. I use the paper-bag technique for all these species. Many of the daisy family have parachutes. As some begin to fly away, I step in and take the remaining ones as they're getting ready for their maiden voyage. Again, straight into a paper bag with them.

MONDAY 26 JULY

A couple of years ago I stuck in a couple of stout willow poles to support a tumbledown wattle panel. Needless to say, they took root and have become quite substantial, in fact they tower over the surrounding hedge. When I went over to them earlier, I was astonished to find that hornets had stripped some of the bark from the stems and were feasting on what I can only imagine was sugary sap. Of course, willows are the source of aspirin, so it could be that they had a headache and were self-medicating.

OPPOSITE I collect seed on dry days. It's a low-tech activity, all that's needed is a few paper bags, a pen and a pair of scissors.

Life in a Cottage Garden

WEDNESDAY 28 JULY

Although most of my garden is planted permanently, with its feet in the ground, I love the idea of using containers here and there as moveable feasts which can alter and affect the feel of any area.

Container growing has become part and parcel of British gardening. From the simple terracotta pots of back-door patios to the grand cast-iron urns of country mansions or the half-barrels of rural homesteads, the container is an institution. Some use it as a chance to experiment, others as an opportunity to repeat past successes. Sometimes it is pressed into use continuously, summer bedding following a winter/spring display of pansies and wallflowers. Most often it presents an opening to use tender plants with gay abandon – pelargoniums, fuchsia and verbena, or for the more adventurous, cannas, phormiums and dahlias.

One group of plants, though, is rarely thought of as suitable for containers, but I use them all the time. Herbaceous perennials have been used in increasingly imaginative ways during the last few decades in beds and borders, but they are seldom considered in the context of containers. Preparing plants for flower shows for sixteen years I noticed how some perennials lend themselves to pot culture, whilst for others it is anathema. As a general rule, fibrous-rooted subjects, cranesbills and the like, are perfectly happy growing in pots. Tap-rooted plants, anchusa and verbascums, don't take kindly to being confined unless they have ample room to send their long roots ever downwards.

I love to use perennials. They are so versatile. Most are hardy and easy to care for. Dead-heading and the removal of dead leaves is all the tending they will need. I make sure they are well watered and I give them an occasional liquid feed with a balanced organic product.

Providing they are planted in containers of adequate volume in a loam-based compost which will provide sustenance for a long time, they will give years of reward without the constant need to hoick plants in and out and renew compost.

Perennials do what it says on the packet. Well chosen, they can last for years. They can be as impactful as any temporary show and their possible combinations are endless. What is more, you can split and divide plants already in the garden and put them together in ways you have never used before.

This year I'm experimenting with a combination I've not tried before. It's a simple recipe: three plants each of *Patrinia scabiosifolia*, a tall valerian relative with vivid, citric-yellow flowers, and a lovely *Agastache rugosa* with golden leaves and purple flowers called 'Golden Jubilee'. Both are terrific plants for attracting beneficial insects to far-flung corners of the garden. And that is the whole point about growing plants in containers; you can put them wherever they are needed.

OPPOSITE *Pots of perennials can be hefty but they will last for the rest of the summer and into the autumn. Choosing subjects with good seedheads is a good way of prolonging the season.*
BELOW *The big* Patrinia scabiosifolia *in the pot, started life as maverick seedlings in a tray of echeveria.*

July
Eryngium

At summer's peak, rounded clumps of herbaceous
perennials are very satisfying in a border, rather like a room full of plump
women all dolled up for a party. But their curvaceous image is made all the
more reassuring by a contrast or two. A few spiky characters can provide just
what is needed, and none does it more effectively than eryngium.

Sea-hollies are a spiny, prickly bunch; they give parts of the garden here
a frisson, take them away and garden life would be more mundane, more
humdrum. All over the top of the garden at Glebe Cottage, *Eryngium bourgatii*
abounds. It is in its element in the sunny borders and raised beds in this
part of the garden, seeding itself amongst the crumbling brick paths and
occasionally finding a foothold between stones in the low walls that support
the little terraces.

All sea-hollies create a sense of anticipation, and *Eryngium bourgatii* does it
best! Its summer season may begin as early as May, when flower stems start to
emerge from basal rosettes of leaves. The rosettes themselves are splendid
throughout the year, much cut and glaucous, with veins and midribs lined
with white, as though an unseen hand had tipped quicksilver on each leaf,
but however eye-catching they may be, this is just a prelude to the
flowerheads.

OPPOSITE AND BELOW
Our blue form of
Eryngium bourgatii
*is a great favourite with
insects. Sometimes it is
difficult to see the flowers
because of the wealth of
insects gathered there to
feed and forage.*

The individual flowers of all eryngiums are tiny, clustered together to
form columns, spheres or cones, and, in the case of most Eurasian species,
surrounded by big, showy bracts, fiercely armed with spikes. Such defences
have evolved to deter grazing animals intent on predation; they protect both
flowers and the seeds which follow them and which, when ripe, drop into the
spiky chalice. In the arid areas most of these plants inhabit, all leaves are fair
game, but even the hungriest goat would shrink from tackling a spiky clump
of *Eryngium bourgatii* on a sun-baked Pyrennean hillside.

These menacing and highly visible armaments constitute the plant's major
attraction for gardeners, not just in their architecture but also in their
transforming colours. Most start green, a glaucous green barely discernible
from the leaves, but as they head upwards they become silver, until the whole
flower head takes on a reflective shimmer. Many sea-hollies, especially forms
of *Eryngium bourgatii*, don't stop there; gradually, almost before your eyes,
stems, bracts and flowers become brilliant blue as though the plant had
imbibed ultramarine ink. It is this colour change more than any other factor
that makes *Eryngium bourgatii* such a desirable plant, avidly sought after by those
who see it for the first time.

I have always yearned to grow true sea-holly, *Eryngium maritimum*. I've even
tried to tempt it into my garden by luring it with beds of pure sand and
perfect drainage, but it wouldn't oblige. You could almost hear it yearning
for the smell of the sea and the taste of salt spray on its waxy, heavily
armoured bracts. Struggling against the tide is a little pointless anyway
when I can jump in the car in July, drive fifteen miles and see it in all its
prickly glory where it is truly at home in the sand dunes.

Life in a Cottage Garden

August

August is a stop-start sort of a month. Some years it is hot, so hot you wish you could forget about everything and just drink-in the sunshine. What a thrill to put your bare feet down on the slates on the terrace and feel them burning, to have to scurry for the shade to cool them down or work out the least searing route to your straw mat, arranged carefully to make the most of the sun. Such days start with low mist, the early sun streaming through the trees, moisture hanging in the air. As the sun climbs high in the sky the mood changes, the birds whose song resounded in the wood this morning are quiet now. The fledglings practising their flight and arguing with each other fall silent.

By midday there is a sizzling torpor, it's easy to persuade yourself there is nothing to do – but that is never the case in a garden. True, everything has expanded as much as it is going to. Plants will never be more voluminous, flowers will never be fuller or brighter than they are during August.

In the early part of the month the pace of the garden speeds up to a noisy crescendo. 'Keep it coming' could be the clarion call for the dog days of August. There is more

OPPOSITE In the woodland garden early morning sunlight streams in. On occasions like this individual plants, even trees, are forgotten in the magnitude of the moment, not to mention its magic.
ABOVE Dianella tasmanica *has set a fine crop of its rich blue berries this year. Herbaceous plants with berries are exciting — especially when they're blue.*

156   *Life in a Cottage Garden*

harvesting than sowing now and the fresh verdancy of May has given way to saturated green splashes here and there with vibrant colour as tomatoes and peppers begin to redden and squashes and pumpkins start to ripen. At the same time, French and runner beans hang down, showing off their handsome pods, alongside borlotto beans, so handsomely marbled, purple beans and the gorgeous waxy pods of 'Cornetti Meraviglia di Venezia', a glorious yellow bean just made for salads.

This is the month of the harvest moon, and there are long balmy evenings to sit out and eat, enjoying the garden and its bounty. It is fruition time. There is so much to harvest; you can allow yourself the indulgence of paper-thin shaved fennel for salads, courgette flowers stuffed with fragrant rice and herb-flecked artichoke hearts sitting in tepid olive oil. On holiday in your own garden.

Watering, feeding, tidying and clearing are the order of the day now. The combination of hot days and plenty of rain means that growth has hardly slowed down. Agapanthus reach their peak. Most have survived the rigours of last winter and it seems their flowering is all the more abundant for the cold they have endured. There are lashings of flowers, big splashes of colour.

Exotics are at their best in the latter part of the year and many are already climbing towards their peak now. The garden has reached its zenith.

Views enjoyed for weeks begin to disappear behind curtains of fennel, sweet pea stems laden with flower and tropical and sub-tropical visitors determined to make the most of the season. Dahlias, cannas and gingers hot up the tempo.

There is rain too; a sudden summer storm can turn the sky yellow and black and lay the garden to waste in an afternoon, but as the clouds recede and the sun begins to shine, puddles evaporate and the paths and terrace begin to steam. (In the event, this was one of the coolest Augusts for many years.)

MONDAY 2 AUGUST

One of August's most iconic plants in my garden is agapanthus. For years after we came here I thought it would be impossible to grow these gorgeous South African lilies, but I was encouraged to give them a try by my friend Richard Lee from Rosemoor, who started me off with a few of his own seedlings, grown from named Headbourne hybrids. They have proved to be totally hardy when they are in the ground and I have had the thrill of collecting seed from them and selecting my own plants, many of which now grace the garden. When one seedling stands out, perhaps for the depth of the colour of its flowers, their shape or its bearing, I divide it when it is big enough to make more of something special. Agapanthus increase fairly fast and divisions can be returned to the ground, but they probably make up into bigger plants more quickly if they are potted up.

OPPOSITE *On hot days Sylvie, one of our two cats, doesn't know what to do with herself. Whereas the dogs find some shade, she seems to prefer hotspots, especially if there's a lizard to taunt.*

BELOW *Agapanthus seedheads are just as beautiful as the flowers. Their elegant structures last for months, eventually turning dry and biscuit-coloured.*

THURSDAY 5 AUGUST

I probably ought to stake more often that I do. Plants in the borders here grow in such close proximity that most of the time they hold each other up. The fact that I always choose species, or cultivars that are close to the species, helps. They are almost always stronger than over-bred hybrids. When it comes to asters I avoid the countless cultivars of *Aster novae-belgii*. I did try, but they always succumbed to mildew, their foliage looking almost ghostly, and because we garden organically there was nothing to be done. Instead I plump for cultivars which are really close to the wild plants. Many are waist-high and produce clouds of bloom, but I have a soft spot for *Aster* 'Calliope' and I've included it in the new planting in Annie's border, where its dark stems and leaves will make a good contrast to white cosmos and pale geraniums. It is very tall, as tall as me, and though its stems are robust, in this, its first year in this new position, I must give it a chance and stake it. Not until October will we enjoy the benefit of its big blue daisies, hopefully held aloft rather than prostrate.

SUNDAY 8 AUGUST

Dark-leaved bananas have been a focal point in our hot borders for the last few years. Though the plants were still in pots they had made magnificent specimens, but last winter, despite being kept in the protection of a tunnel, they died. I turned them out of the pots onto a trolley wrapped up in thick black plastic, expecting to discover a solid base on the plant and at least a few roots. The base was squidgy – there were no roots – it was stone dead. The plastic looked like a body bag and the corpse was carried to the compost heap. Sometimes when a plant dies in your garden or your tunnel it's not a good idea to try again, but with bananas it's always a calculated risk and any gardener who tries to grow tropical subjects understands that cold winters may bring devastation. But when you've seen how magnificent these plants look, you're hooked and you just have to have another go. Even if there are multiple deaths, you persist. Neil is giving me a hand to carry out the new bananas. They already have huge, dark, glossy leaves and as we lower the first one into a big copper pot in the hot borders I know I'm doing the right thing.

TUESDAY 10 AUGUST

Phew. All that effort early in the year sorting out *Clematis* 'Huldine', disentangling it from the crab apple and resetting it in a more civilised manner, has paid off. Not only is the crab apple looking happier (it was full of blossom and now its fruit is just beginning to take colour), but the clematis is flowering prolifically and by the look of the multitude of buds, there are masses of flowers still to come. It should still be flowering in October.

The renowned plantsman Graham Stuart-Thomas was once asked to look at a border which its owners felt was failing aesthetically. It was beautifully cultivated and immaculately maintained, colours blended seamlessly along its length, but something was not working. Eventually, having pondered for some time, Mr Stuart-Thomas realised that its problem was the scale of its foliage – there was nothing wrong with the leaves that were there, but they were all the same size.

In a border or even a large container a range of scale, form, colour and texture is vital. The factor most commonly overlooked is scale.

Sometimes we become obsessed with the form of plants, we want spikes and spires, broad drifts, focal points. We consider colour schemes, vivid and tropical, pale and pastel or subdued and subtle. In any border foliage is the main component. From March or April through to October or November, almost all its constituents will be in leaf and the size of that foliage and its relationship with the leaves of neighbouring plants is always going to be of primary importance.

There are plenty of plants with smaller leaves. True, there is infinite variation in their shape and colour, but finding perennials and annuals that add drama and pzazz needs careful thought. Miss Jekyll recognised the importance of including large-leaved plants in her schemes. In fact, several of the signature plants that occur over and over in her highly detailed plans have big, bold foliage. Most large-leaved plants enjoy a rich living – many gather moisture – but there are others, often silver or grey covered in fine, furry velvet that tolerate much drier conditions. There are hardy plants happy in shade and moist conditions which provide volume and drama – hostas, rodgersias and ligularias. Many of the tropical plants I include in the hot borders have large, lush leaves which grow rapidly once the weather warms up. They need cosseting and lifting in and out of winter quarters but, providing they have protection and temperatures don't plummet too low, they can be wheeled out to bring some magic where it is needed.

There are never enough of them, though, and in my hot borders I need one plant with big presence and huge leaves that I can repeat throughout the borders. *Ricinus communis* fits the bill perfectly. Plants of the dark-leaved form which I sowed in February and potted on in May have grown astronomically and I'm carrying them out for their summer season. Immediately they are plonked into place, their pots disguised amongst the dense undergrowth, and the border takes on an exotic air underlined by the bananas, cannas and ornamental gingers. Maximum impact from minimal expense, they will stay in the border, joined by vivid daisies emphasising their scale and stature. They will be watered and fed occasionally, growing bigger and better until the frost and autumn gales dishevel their handsome leaves and cut them down to size.

OPPOSITE *Dropping these huge ricinus into the hot borders makes for instant impact.*
BELOW *I'm glad I grew so many of these Rudbeckia 'Rustic Dwarfs' from seed. They provide an under-storey of burning embers, making the whole border sizzle.*

OPPOSITE AND BELOW

These big square pots on the way down the garden make good stopping-off points to view the borders on either side. They need to look well-turned out at all times.

SATURDAY 14 AUGUST

The way in which every part of the garden changes throughout the year is a source of constant joy and entertainment. It's exciting, especially if I've been away for a week, to turn a corner and survey a scene where new flowers have arrived. I am certainly no mistress of successional planting, but I always aspire to creating a garden where plants take over from each other in a subtle and seamless way. It will probably never happen.

Growing plants in pots and containers calls for a more concerted effort. Decisions have to be definite. There is no room for the random intervention of self-seeders or unexpected surprises. There are three pairs of large square pots at intervals on the way down the garden and if they share the same planting schemes it lends some cohesion to these beds below the hot borders.

But I love to ring the changes. In November they are planted up with tulips. This year it was *T.* 'Purissima', a huge bowl-shaped flower changing gradually from ivory to white. When its petals had dropped, that was it. I replaced it with plants of a dark-leaved *Eucomis comosa*, at that time a collection of basal rosettes of dark purpley leaves. Around them I added young plants of *Cerinthe major* 'Purpurascens', a plant I've used this year in several containers around the garden.

Both eucomis and cerinthe were raised from seed, the latter sown earlier this year, but the eucomis is now three or four years old. Its seed was collected from my big handsome plants of *E. comosa* 'Sparkling Burgundy', some of my most treasured bulbs. I was hoping that my seedlings might flower this year and, sure enough, they have. The colour of the leaves is not so deep and consistent as the named form, but I think they are beautiful and I am really proud of them. When the cerinthe was in full flower, its dark bracts echoed the colour of the eucomis leaves. Now it has become a bit straggly, and I need to smarten up the pots, so out it comes. It has set seed already and I will collect some of this en route to the compost heap. In its stead, I am going to replant with a soft wispy grass, *Stipa tenuissima,* and pretty geranium *G. wallichianum* 'Buxton's Variety', which has azure blue chalices with a white centre and marbled leaves which turn crimson in the autumn. It also has a rambling habit, so the plan is that it will soften the edges of the pots and both it and the grass will enhance the eucomis as its flower stems lengthen and its colour deepens.

Later, the set will change again. Although eucomis can sometimes survive even a cold winter outdoors, my bulbs are much too precious to risk it. In October I will take the pots apart once more. The eucomis will be potted in good compost and join their parents underneath the staging in the greenhouse to rest for the winter. They will have one good watering and then not be watered again until the spring. Next year they may find themselves in a completely different venue, perhaps in individual clay pots, placed at the edge of steps or a path. Wherever they turn up, they'll be beautiful.

Monday 16 August

Gladioli are a divisive issue amongst gardeners. The main bone of contention is simply whether or not they should be given a place in our gardens. When we first moved here, more than thirty years ago, I had no choice. A few tall stems of vibrant magenta flowers suddenly appeared in the midst of the tangle of weeds we were hoping to convert into a garden. They were close to the cottage, giving the impression that at some stage they might actually have been planted there. They had the same structure and similar flowers to the gladioli grown in rigid rows in the vegetable gardens and allotments of my youth, but there the resemblance ended. These were relaxed, laid-back flowers with a natural grace and elegance never encountered in the stiff spikes of the florists' gladioli popularised by Dame Edna Everage. There's no doubt that amongst the naturalistic gardening lobby, gladioli have had a very negative press, yet many eminent gardeners, not least Christopher Lloyd and Beth Chatto, have championed the cause of some branches of the family, especially the species and the smaller-flowered cultivars.

Our magenta gladiolus, eventually identified as *G. communis* subsp. *byzantinus*, is still in residence here and increases rapidly now that the garden is slightly more civilised, entirely disregarding the blue and yellow colour scheme I tried to impose on the bed where it grows. It crops up all over the place, not surprising since it traditionally often grows in scrub or cultivated arable land.

There is a gladiolus in our seaside bed, which also spreads itself around, but I could never have too much of it. *Gladiolus papilio* Purpureoauratus Group loves well-drained 'crunchy' soil, though it has managed to cope with several cold wet winters. It meanders around, colonising new areas with its slender glaucous swords held aggressively upright. The flowers are delightful, if a touch bizarre, of a subtle greyish purple. The buds are fat, like nothing so much as a tropical fish, and open to a soft bell shape, the two lower petals exquisitely marked with circles of maroon and yellow, like the spots on a butterfly's wings – hence the 'papilio' part of its title.

Tuesday 17 August

Way back in March, when branches were bare and it seemed like nothing would ever grow again, I pruned the *Cotinus coggyria* 'Grace' that occupies one corner of the hot beds. It is always handsome in leaf, but its wood is prone to snapping, especially in this rather windy position. With a sharp pair of secateurs I removed all the damaged wood and cut back the framework hard so that each of the laterals had only two or three buds. Thanks to this, it has burgeoned. In fact, it's grown so well that the rudbeckia and crocosmias planted in waves underneath it are in danger of suffering light deprivation. Something's got to give, and once more I have to step in with the secateurs.

OPPOSITE *Despite its quiet and subtle colouring,* Gladiolus papilio Purpureoauratus Group *enchants those who have never seen it before; while those who have are already under its spell.*
BELOW *Though I don't usually go in for Dame Edna gladioli, a pale green and a dark red variety were effective in pots on the path through the hot border.*

BELOW *Brimstone
butterflies usually visit the
garden in May, but by
August they are building
up energy for hibernation,
sucking nectar wherever
they can find it.*
OPPOSITE *I don't really
dress to match my plants!*

WEDNESDAY 18 AUGUST

I always grow a few sweet peas, more for their scent than anything, and the one that smells sweetest is *Lathyrus odoratus* 'Cupani'. I usually sow the seeds in the autumn, but this year I overlooked it and the seeds weren't sown until the beginning of March. Instead of planting them out in their usual position amongst climbing French beans, they have pride of place as the sole occupants in two large iron pots. Neil got our local blacksmith to make simple iron supports which fit exactly inside the pots. I've used these to wind round a sort of macrame structure of garden twine, and since I sever all the tendrils to increase flower quality, tying them in to this offers the support they need. There are only four plants in each pot, but thanks to old muck and rich compost the sweet peas are exceptionally good. It's always a good idea to cut flowers constantly to encourage more to grow, which means I have the pleasure of big bunches in the kitchen every day.

FRIDAY 20 AUGUST

Seed saving goes on in earnest during August. It's not always a question of waiting for a whole plant to finish flowering – there are some plants which set seed and yet continue to flower for months on end. Calendulas are like this. Although the seed can be collected at any time, it's always the best practice to take seed from some of the first flowers that were produced. They tend to be the biggest and the best. It stands to sense, really, that a plant's first flowers and its seeds are its insurance policy: the sooner it can set them, the sooner they will make new plants. *Calendula officinalis* 'Indian Prince' is the one that I have all over the garden and use in rows amongst my vegetables as a companion plant.

SUNDAY 22 AUGUST

Each time I see a butterfly alight on a flower I'm reminded that this is not my garden. It's communal, shared with a plethora of insects, reptiles, small mammals and birds, not to mention all the invisible life forms that live in the soil. We tend to assume that flowers have somehow evolved just for our enjoyment. It has nothing to do with us. Brightly coloured petals and delicious perfumes are there simply to lure pollinating insects. It's all about sex.

I try to include as wide a variety of different flower shapes and structures as possible – different sizes too – many have a special relationship with specific insects. Whenever possible, native plants are encouraged; they are bound to suit native wildlife best. When it comes to nectar, though, butterflies are not fussy, they will drink at any bar, but as far as laying their eggs and the food supply for their larvae, access to native plants is essential. Nettles and brambles are high up on the menu.

Everyone recognises teasels. *Dipsacus fullonum* is majestic. Although it repels anything that tries to eat it, it does provide food in abundance for bees and other insects and seed for the birds during winter. The tiny flowers that compose the prickly, ovoid heads open in rows in succession, so nectar is available over a long period. As if that were not generous enough, water collects in the little basins created at the junction between stem and leaf, and birds come to drink.

These symbiotic relationships between insects and flowers benefit both parties equally; food is provided and pollen carried, seed is set, goldfinches move in, and in the process of gorging on the rich harvest, they spill surplus seed that then germinates and begins the process all over again.

Tuesday 24 August

There are several woods close by Glebe Cottage which must at one time have been coppiced. Tall, dangly branches emanate from hazel stumps; ancient bases entangled with honeysuckle drip with moss and lichen. The ground underneath them is no longer disturbed by the woodsman's boots: the only visitors here are occasional deer, a fox and a badger or two. The ground is thick with the leaf litter from a hundred autumns, the ideal conditions for the wood anenome. When we first came to the garden there were very few plants, apart from rough grass – mainly couch – and an abundance of nettles and bramble, but tucked into one of the hedgerows was a big patch of wood anenomes. We came to the house in July, so it was not until the next spring that they showed their pretty faces.

Although they are amongst the most successful of colonising plants, I always want to make more and this is the best time to do it. There is no visible sign of them above ground, but I only have to move an inch or so of earth before I discover patches of their rhizomes wending their way through the soil. Increasing them is a simple process. I break the rhizomes into chunks, the length of my little finger; as long as each one has a small resting bud and a good piece of rhizome, it has everything it needs to make a whole new plant. If a new colony is to be established then I'll arrange around twenty pieces a few inches apart in a shallow hole incorporating lashings of leaf mould. I water them in, and forget about them until next spring.

Wednesday 25 August

Collecting seed can be such a hit-and-miss affair. Sometimes the weather conspires against you and the seed you have been cherishing is sodden and rots. On other occasions, seed has done what it's supposed to, and distributed itself. I am too late. When I see something really special, an aquilegia with extra-long spurs, or a particularly pretty hepatica, instead of just imagining I will remember which it is when the time comes to collect

OPPOSITE *It's a prickly business tying on bits of ribbon to eryngiums, but it will be well worth it to keep the blue and the purple separate.*
BELOW *Each of these little rhizomes should make a flowering plant by next spring.*

BELOW *Even before they
lose their two outer shells,
the seedpods of* Lunaria
rediviva *are translucent.
Preceding these elegant
seedpods were graceful
white flowers.*
OPPOSITE *Sylvie loves it
when I sit down. My lap is
much more comfortable
than the sleepers.*

seed, I try to mark it with a piece of coloured thread and, if I'm feeling particularly efficient, to write a note to myself as an aide-memoire. There are two very disctinctive *Eryngium bourgatii* in a border by the top terrace. One is brilliant blue, the other deep purple. I tie on my ribbons and make a note.

THURSDAY 26 AUGUST

The marbled leaves of *Arum italicum* 'Pictum' will soon start to push through the ground, but its old flower stems are now wrapped round with green berries and some of them are just changing to orange and red. They stand to attention in little groups here and there through the garden. They are a favourite with the blackbirds but I'm stealing a few to grow new plants for other parts of the garden. I rub the flesh off the berries between my thumb and forefinger. When Sylvie gets off my knee, I'll wash the berries thoroughly to remove all traces of the flesh and push the seeds individually into a seed tray of gritty compost so that they are well covered. I'll finish off with a layer of grit and take the tray into the greenhouse, where they will germinate rapidly. Should I decide there is no hurry, I'll just put them outside.

Only a few other perennial plants produce berries. *Dianella tasmanica* has the most unusual bright-blue berries that look like jewels suspended from its stems by under-employed pixies. Our native *Iris foetidissima,* unflatteringly known as the stinking iris, is still fairly widespread in the British countryside. It adores alkaline soils and in some areas makes vast enclaves, seeding itself around freely and making larger and larger colonies. Its seeds are probably its most outstanding feature: large and orange, they burst out of the fat seed pods during November and December, often remaining in fine fettle deep into the winter. At a time of year when colour is so lacking, it makes an important feature at the edge of the woodland garden. The handsome deep-green arrow heads of *Arum italicum* with their white marbling cover the ground close by, some of them planted deliberately, but most of them self-seeded. They form a wonderful winter combination with architectural clumps of the iris' sharp, shiny evergreen leaves.

FRIDAY 27 AUGUST

Few flowers are cultivated specifically for their seedheads. The silver moons of honesty are so breathtaking in the winter garden that they are reason enough to grow and treasure the plant. Each is composed of three paper-thin discs with the flat seeds trapped between the layers. As winter weather erodes the outside layers, the seeds fall to the ground to create a new generation. Occasionally the whole disc rolls away in the wind like some demented wheel, only to lodge itself in an unpropitious corner. The following year, infant plants will spring up and in the next May there will be strong stems laden with crucifer flowers in rich purple or pure white. As the summer

progresses, they will be replaced by slender seed pods, changing gradually to the familiar discs. As they stretch and dry they fade through sea-green to parchment. Both annual honesty, *Lunaria annua*, and its perennial cousin *Lunaria rediviva*, which has elliptical seed pods, set and distribute seed in the same way. As they lose their outside coatings, their fragile shells assume a translucent quality; caught in a glancing shaft of low sun, they light up even the darkest reaches of the winter garden.

SUNDAY 29 AUGUST

Sometimes I have to set aside a day to catch up with all my cuttings and seedlings. Although I'm in my element in the midst of them, I still have to steel myself and shun all distractions. At this time of year, just leaving young plants for a few days can result in disaster. Propagation isn't just about the excitement of sowing seed or taking cuttings, it's all about the nurture you're prepared to offer your young plants when they've done you the ultimate honour of germinating or taking root.

MONDAY 30 AUGUST

One of the most exciting challenges in gardening is planning planting schemes that will continue colour and interest right through the year, or at least through the great majority of it. 'Painting a picture with plants' is a term often applied to gardening, but rather than meriting comparisons with two- or even three-dimensional art, the most striking analogy is with film. Here though, the credits never roll, the picture constantly moves, it is ever changing. But how to plan it, how to continue the colour and excitement throughout the year? This has to be one of the most challenging yet rewarding dilemmas any gardener faces.

For me and lots of modern gardeners, the season is as close to all-the-year-round as we can manage. Thinking of how plants will change and what each of their changes will mean visually is exciting. As I'm writing this it all sounds marvellously organised, not to mention successful, as an idea, but the reality is much more hit and miss. Not only is there plenty of room for my plans to go awry – never enough time, too many conflicting loyalties and too many areas to keep tabs on – but the ever-present vagaries of weather and season can throw a few spanners in the works too. There have been some unexpected weather events this year; August has been cool and changeable.

What may work perfectly in one year may fail in another, but along the way there are unexpected surprises, unimagined effects and accidental loveliness that make the whole thing worthwhile and that add a new dimension to gardening efforts. Above all my policy is to be adventurous and to have fun, it does not matter if plans do not always work out. It's gardening; it goes on and on.

OPPOSITE *Thank goodness I've got a nursery full of plants and can fill in, change things round and add vital colour when there is a pressing need for it.*
BELOW Crocosmia *'Amberglow' epitomises August's drift into September.*

August
Crocosmias

At this time of year, plants that match the mood of the moment, zooming up the colour scale to reach the highest notes with simmering reds and upbeat yellows, are worth their weight in gold. If they are self-reliant and robust, all the more reason to welcome them into the garden. Crocosmias are always treated hospitably here, especially in our hot borders.

This year they have flourished despite some early setbacks. Their foliage is lush and their blooms more consequential than usual. Like so many South African plants of the iris family, they benefit from copious amounts of water and plenty of warmth during their summer growing period.

Most of us are familiar with 'montbretia', *Crocosmia* x *crocosmiiflora*. It must have been thrown away by the ton since it was introduced as a novelty from the French nursery Lemoine in the 1880s. Small wonder that so many road verges, hedgerows and waste places up and down the country host generous displays of its burnt orange flowers.

All crocosmia spread by making chains of corms like big 1960s beads. New corms are produced at the top of the chain and it is these plump, fresh corms that make flowers. In the wild they would perpetually access new ground, but in the confines of a garden clumps move round in ever-decreasing circles, becoming congested and barren.

To maximise flower size and quality, they should be lifted every two years in spring, breaking off the fat new top corms and replanting them 5–10 centimetres deep – having added home-made compost or any other organic matter to the soil. When I replant them, I'm not shy about it. Crocosmias love a throng. We plant them in great waves, amongst other perennials to mingle at will or in resounding swathes of one variety to make undeniable impact. But I only use the new top corms, discarding the old ones.

Most crocosmias are hardy just about anywhere in the British Isles providing they are given a good thick mulch. All our crocosmias here at Glebe Cottage shot into growth early this year and were then hammered by a severe late frost. Such a shame, since their fresh, young, vertical leaves are one of the delights of spring. Although they looked dishevelled at first, recovery was rapid and they are all coming into flower now, none the worse for it.

Crocosmias fit well into the modern garden. Their informal, wandering growth is ideal in naturalistic schemes. I'm not the sort of person who likes everything in its allotted space and I have a fondness for laid-back, spontaneous plants. Crocosmias have a mind of their own and a wandering spirit. Their vividly coloured flowers (there is no such thing as a subtle crocosmia) lend a touch of the exotic and their sword-like foliage, either in bright green or occasionally in bronze, makes a useful contribution from April onwards. In the low early-spring light, leaves are translucent and add an element of movement amongst static clumps of geraniums and other perennials, but it is now that their vivid flowers set the garden alight.

Whether they accompany fiery rudbeckia or pale lilac phlox or simply stand on their own, they are the spirit of the August garden.

OPPOSITE
Crocosmia Walberton *Yellow is new to the garden and one of the prettiest. Its flowers of soft, warm yellow look well with its narrow mid-green leaves. The mahogany rudbeckia is a perfect neighbour.*
BELOW *Crocosmia 'Flame' is one of the first to flower. Sturdy, with compact spikes of really red flowers, it quickly increases to make solid clumps.*

Life in a Cottage Garden

September

The garden party reaches the height of its festivity in autumn. There is luscious colour and the gorgeous warm scent of fruit at its ripest, mixes with a lingering waft of the Mediterranean, thyme and cistus – a reprise of the summer on warm afternoons. Jangling cannas and exuberant dahlias jostle to outdo each other in the grand finale. Yet somehow there is no rush. The autumn is its own time, not a corridor between summer and winter. Red admirals lazily suck the sweetness from the blackest of blackberries, the fields hum with harvest home, the hedges are thick with rose hips and the vivid red berries of twining bryony. Flowers lounge around, huge sheets of rudbeckia blaze away, made all the sunnier by a splash of blue from the very first Michaelmas daisies. On cooler evenings the smell of a wood fire mingles with the aroma of damp earth, and the first of the funghi erupt at the woodland's edge.

September is full of contradictions, fulfillment and decay. Colchicums burst out amongst the remnants of their old, dishevelled leaves. *Colchicum speciosum* 'Album' has to epitomise this unexpected genesis. Under the beeches,

OPPOSITE *September's borders are thick with life. Flowers and foliage crowd together in a busy melee.* ABOVE *A red admiral sleepily sips on the nectar of a rudbeckia flower. This is a time of plenty.*

tinged with the first russet evidence of change, the great white chalices of anemones open alongside the pale lemon bells of kirengeshoma. The bare ground, bereft since the departure of the early flowers, is suddenly alive with the tiny flags of the first cyclamen.

A gang of long-tailed tits arrive suddenly in the uppermost branches of the purple bird cherry, *Prunus padus* 'Colorata', that stands opposite one of the bedroom windows. I'm lucky enough to be close to the window as they fly in noisily. Their chattering is instantly recognisable as they move through the garden, stopping here and there to catch a few aphids, digressing to examine flowers they have never investigated before. But they love the *Prunus padus*; it always seems to be their final destination within the garden before they make off noisily to the high hazel hedge behind the house, then on along the hedgerows and across the fields. Their visit is brief but always joyful, and before they leave their acrobatics are enough to dislodge quantities of leaves, to make a pretty litter of pink and purple lining the path and settling in the tops of *Helenium* 'Lemon Queen'. I realise with a sinking feeling that so many leaves have already fallen from the branches you can see straight through the framework of the tree.

Overhead in a clear blue sky, swallows gather to practise aeronautics for their imminent departure. Though they are gathering for their exodus, some must already have left. Nonetheless, a few persevere, warming up for the long journey ahead. Their aerobatic displays are phenomenal.

Migrations are happening in all directions. A few weeks ago a small group of ravens returned to their winter and spring haunt in two huge Scots pines in the hedgerow behind the house. On a clear, crisp evening with big pink clouds, the trees are silhouetted against the darkening sky as the ravens return to their roosts, making their strangely evocative, croaking call.

The temperature is so noticeably different now, almost cold. In contrast the fast-fading sun turns the big cumulus cascading over the horizon to warmest apricot.

WEDNESDAY 1 SEPTEMBER

There's a small apple tree near the pond at the bottom of the garden. It was given to me by one of the boys I used to teach when he'd left school and gone to work at a truly wonderful nursery here that specialised in local apples. They had more than 200 varieties. He turned up one day with this tree as a present. It was a chuck-out, a bit of a strange shape, but a sweet little tree. He told me it was grown on a dwarfing rootstock and, sure enough, even after thirty years it's still a small tree – with a big stretch I can reach most of the apples that decorate its branches. It's a 'Discovery', a variety whose fruit doesn't keep particularly but has some of the reddest apples you ever saw, and when you bite into the sweet white flesh you are amazed to find it suffused with pink. Everyone has a picture of a rosy apple, and 'Discovery' has to be

OPPOSITE *The chaff from these sunflower heads falls away easily, revealing perfect spirals of seed.* BELOW *Annie's apple tree is groaning under the weight of the biggest crop ever.*

the archetypal rosy apple. In most springs it repays me with a bounty of lovely white and pink flowers, hopefully followed by an abundant crop of fruit. When it flowers in May, frost is still a spectre, and though it is unlikely to damage the blossom it can jeopardise pollination. Not this year. Neil's bees had just arrived when it came into flower. No sooner had they taken residence and made themselves at home in the garden than they were off to forage in the apple trees. They were their first port of call. A bee-line? So this year the tree is laden.

My little apple tree is very well travelled. It has been to the Chelsea Flower Show on more than one occasion – in fact it has been the focus of our exhibit and twice part of a Gold-Medal display. For several years it grew in a pot and was just about transportable. Every year is different – some years blossom was over as D-day approached, some years it was still in bud, but one year it was perfect. It was carefully placed in the lorry – it was the last thing to go in, for weeks before I had zealously protected it, making sure it would be in pristine condition for the big event. When we got to Chelsea late in the evening and the lorry was opened, to my dismay several shelves had tumbled down. In the twilight I could discern squashed plants. I leapt into the lorry, climbed on to a box to survey the damage and promptly fell into the apple tree. I didn't cry, but you've never seen a lorry unloaded so quickly. In the event most of the plants had survived unscathed, the goddess was with us and the apple tree was the star of the show.

FRIDAY 3 SEPTEMBER

In May this year I cleared out a couple of rows of chard from the vegetable garden, raked the soil and sowed a birdseed mix across an area of a few square yards. It was a mixture of different grasses with a large percentage of sunflower seed. I waited diligently for it to germinate. Most of the grass came up, but not one sunflower. I had forgotten that birds were quite liable to help themselves to the tastiest delicacy. Nobody told them to wait.

I station-sowed some of the remaining sunflower seed in module trays. With big seeds like this it's a good idea to sow each seed individually, giving it its own station. When they were sturdy little plants I potted them on, then put them into whacking pots in old potting compost when they reached adolescence. They have made brilliant yellow flowers, and now that their stems have started to dry, I've cut them all, and on this glorious September day I'm removing the chaff and hanging the heads on the bean supports. When they have dried out thoroughly, I'll hang them in the shed and put them out later in the dead of winter, when the birds are really hungry. My experiment wasn't too successful and produced little seed for the birds. We feed our birds huge amounts of seeds, along with nuts and a variety of other foods. To produce enough to be self-sufficient in this would take a lot more land than we have to spare.

Life in a Cottage Garden

SUNDAY 5 SEPTEMBER

It is easy to take the plants in our gardens for granted and to imagine that they have always been around. Our colonial past, coupled with a temperate climate, mean that our gardens contain a collection of plants from all over the world. In some cases, they are now better represented in our gardens than in their native habitats.

At this time of year it is the vanished North American prairies that are most in evidence in many a garden that, like mine, relies heavily on herbaceous perennials for their main early autumn show.

Prairie planting doesn't always seem to have much relevance if you've got a small garden, but the glorious prairie daisies that are often the essence of these big planting schemes are just as useful and equally at home on a smaller scale, as in my brick garden. They are reliability personified: accommodating, and easy to grow and, in most cases, long-lived. Clumps go on for years. Rudbeckias are the archetypal prairie plant – more later!

Echinacea purpurea, the purple coneflower, is very closely related to rudbeckia. It is popular in prairie planting schemes, and equally renowned as a herbal remedy for building up the immune system. In the garden its robust, pinky-purple daisies keep up the colour, especially when their anthers appear, lighting up the bronze central cones with fiery orange. In some plants the petals are almost horizontal, in others gently drooping. Seed-raised plants vary enormously; it's worth growing your own and selecting your own seedlings. There are several named forms available with deep colour or bigger flowers, and a whole newer range of hybrids with orange in their colouring, first bred in Canada. They are vegetatively propagated, usually by micro-propagation. On my heavy clay, *E. purpurea* is not long-lived, it probably needs better drainage than we have. On lighter soil it should last for years.

Over the last few years so many echinacea varieties have been introduced in such a range of mouthwatering colours it makes me want to build a bed with sandy soil and devote it to them. No, I'll just grow them for as long as they last and enjoy them while they're there.

Several other North American daisies exhibit unusual raised centres. Those of helenium are almost spherical, characteristically velvety, dark brown or golden-yellow. They are perfectly complemented by soft, undulating petals which either hang down or stick out vertically, surrounding the central boss like a ballet dancer's tutu. No white or pale pink for them, though. Heleniums are gay and jolly flowers, bright chrome yellow, deep crimson and bronze, or combinations of any or all of these. They flower prolifically and make their mark not by great subtlety but by straightforward flower power.

Helenium 'Moerheim Beauty' is an old variety, but always reliable and floriferous. When I cut it back hard after its summer flowering, it produces another display of its velvet-bronze blooms with their furry brown doorknob middles and goes on until October.

OPPOSITE *The brick garden is full of blue and yellow flowers, but at this time of year there is a shortage of blue in some beds. I'm planting more Aster 'Little Carlow', its such a good doer.*
ABOVE *The rich rusty red of* Helenium *'Moerheim Beauty' fits the September mood perfectly.*

Tuesday 7 September

Occasionally you are aware what a perfect sense of timing plants have, as though they were waiting for a specific window in the gardening year to make an appearance, determined to ensure they get the attention they deserve. Autumn-flowering cyclamen are perhaps the archetypal opportunists. Under the beech trees things are dull – apart from the moss (particularly green after heavy rain last month) and the twisting leaves of polypody, it's all dank earth and dun leaves, but running through them are rivulets of pink and white, the massed flowers of *Cyclamen hederifolium*. Their fat corms have been invisible since their foliage died down in April, gathering succour from the soil, but now with the autumn rain and falling temperatures they are triggered into action, exploiting the vacuum and putting all their energy into flower production.

I lived in Rome for a year, and on a trip to the Abruzzi mountains I came across colonies of *Cyclamen hederifolium* growing amongst beech trees. The huge trees made the cyclamen's tiny pink flowers seem even daintier. cyclamen flowers are wondrous; their scrolled buds are long and narrow, the petals gradually unfurl and pull themselves back. Eventually they fade and the flower stem coils itself round, the seedhead swells and ants carry away the seed.

Flowers open over several weeks, but this is just the start of it. As they fade, the foliage takes the stage. Few plants offer such ornamental foliage with such breathtaking flowers as the ivy-leaved cyclamen. Like human fingerprints, the leaves of every plant are unique, no two are ever the same. Their complex patchwork in every shade of autumnal green is one of late autumn's most spectacular shows.

In essence, *Cyclamen hederifolium* is a shade-lover, evolved with other plants and bulbs to exploit the conditions created by trees and make use of extra light as the canopy thins out – the same canopy that has kept its tubers cool, protecting them from fierce sun through the summer. As leaves fall, light and rain filter through and flowers rush to capitalise; pollinating insects are less frequent now. The fallen leaves gradually rot down, providing the plants with humus-rich leaf mould. Leaves emerge, seed is set, the cycle continues.

Thursday 9 September

Eating the first sweetcorn is one of the best treats autumn has to offer. For weeks I've been squeezing the fattening heads, longing for this moment, but I've resisted the temptation to peel back the green outer cases until today. As I pull back the outside layers on the most promising cob, the kernels are revealed in neat rows and as fat as could be. I plunge in a thumbnail to test its ripeness and – bingo! – milky sap exudes. It's ready and now I must dash to cook it, not forgetting to break off the next biggest head – this mustn't be a selfish treat. As soon as you pick it, sugar starts to turn to starch, so time is of the essence. Come on, Neil, you can have the biggest one.

OPPOSITE This self-perpetuating colony of polypody, cyclamen, moss and leaves needs no interference from me.
BELOW Within a matter of days, the white globes of Colchicum speciosum *'Album' spring up from nowhere. Their purity is unsurpassable.*

Life in a Cottage Garden

Saturday 11 September

The light changes throughout the day in most people's gardens, but here at Glebe Cottage I am extra lucky. Because most of the garden is open and exposed to the elements, and because it is south-facing, we experience the whole gamut of light. First thing in the morning the east light is magical. At midsummer, dawn can be as early as 4.30, and it's worth getting up to enjoy it. Thankfully, it is a little later now, the sun is lower and the light stays softer for longer, and in the evening too the dusk is more gradual.

Around the summer solstice, light can be bright, almost harsh, especially at noon; colours in the garden are difficult to see. This is most true of blues and whites. I try to ensure that most of my blue and white flowers are planted where they can be viewed in shade for at least part of the day. This is an extreme example of how important it can be to consider not just the soil and situation, but also how light will affect your perception of the plants you put in.

This is never a more vital consideration than when trying to find a home for grasses. *Imperata cylindrica* 'Rubra', or Japanese blood grass as it's sometimes gorily called, is a case in point. Its crimson blades are matt and lack-lustre when the weather is dull or if the grass is planted in even light, but on the front of our hot bed, both morning and evening it is transformed. As the early sun hits it, and as the evening sun goes down, it takes on a totally new, dramatic guise; it glows. Although photographers, including Jonathan, love soft, even light, when it comes to taking pictures of golden grasses like the molinia in our brick garden, which is just beginning to change as I write this, bright sun is not a problem, especially when it's backlit – in fact, it's an advantage. The rudbeckia in the wheelbarrow opposite are enhanced by the low evening sun and Jonathan's eye for a beautiful shot. When I plant them I must make sure they will be subject to the same sort of light effect; perhaps they'd look good with the imperata.

Monday 13 September

From early July we've been harvesting courgettes, planted on top of a raised mound through black plastic. This is the same place where I discovered a grass snake in early June. Along the bank were a whole range of different cucurbits – in other words, squashes, pumpkins and a cucumber or two. Their growth has been mind-boggling: not only did their lanky stems and huge leaves cover the entire bank, but they decided to use the willow hedge planted behind them as an extra support and proceeded to colonise it. They have been prolific and are still producing new fruit. I'm collecting some of the medium-sized squashes, we'll be able to eat some of them, but there's no way we can use them all. Some will store, but others must be eaten fairly soon. They make easily transportable edible gifts.

OPPOSITE *Perhaps I should leave these rudbeckia in the barrow so they can be wheeled around all day to be lit to their best advantage.* BELOW *Not only do they taste good and some of them store well, but lots of squashes are entertaining too. These crooknecks look like knobbly birds.*

Wednesday 15 September

Sometimes I'm asked what is my favourite plant. It's always impossible to answer; I do have favourites, but I don't like to talk about them, it seems rude to the others. *Selinum wallichianum* would probably be on most gardeners' top ten list if they grew it, but it is seriously underpublicised. This is partly due to when it flowers – now, in September. We are all too preoccupied with all those prairie daisies and those gorgeous dahlias. Despite myself I know that sometimes I have forgotten all about selinum until, on a day like this, I'm wandering down the path in Alice's garden and I come across it doing its own special thing, quietly and unobtrusively but with maximum poise.

My friend Helen objects to my using the word choice when it comes to plants. She's quite right, and nowadays I try not to use it, but it almost springs to my lips when I'm talking about *Selinum wallichianum*. Everything about it is in perfect proportion and both its deportment and its flowers and foliage are faultless. It helps that it is a species; no human hand has ever manipulated it and tried to make it do something that is not in its nature. Many umbels have ferny leaves, but selinum's foliage is something else. In spring it rises later than most perennials but, once it has decided to get up, it briskly spreads out its first tier to form a neat mat. Each of these basal leaves is intricately divided, like big, deep green doilies, on which it builds floor by floor until, during late summer, its buds emerge. Eventually each head of flowers will branch and each of the branches will support as many as 50 tiny flowers held in an airy globe, but at first the whole thing is held tight within a green bract, a fast-inflating parcel full of potential. Another of its virtues is its ability always to flatter whatever is growing alongside. In Alice's garden there are the early buds of a pretty pink schizostylis, the dark-red leaves of peonies and sanguisorbas in their autumnal dress.

There are several plants in the brick garden too. *Crocosmia* 'Star of the East' came up alongside one selinum, and the association of its big orange flowers, with just a touch of mango sorbet, the vivid green of the selinum's foliage and its crimson stems was so perfect that I mean to copy the combination next year in a few other places.

Friday 17 September

Catmint makes a perfect edging for formal borders, but I want to use waves of it running through Annie's garden. There are already several healthy plants there, but I want more. So I'm taking cuttings. This is *Nepeta* 'Six Hills Giant', a buxom variety smothered in purple flowers from May until November, and hugely attractive to insects. Neil's bees have loved it. Heel cuttings work well. I'm detaching a whole module tray's worth, about fifty, neatening them at the base and nipping out the tops. They should root within a month in the sandy, well-drained compost I'm using, sitting on the heated bench.

OPPOSITE *As well as playing an important role amongst other members of the border brigade, all umbels deserve close scrutiny to marvel at the perfection of their structure.*
ABOVE *It's impossible to have too much catmint. It is an insect magnet and flowers for months.*

Life in a Cottage Garden

Sunday 19 September

It's Sunday, so we have the garden to ourselves. The day is golden, it seems to encapsulate all those feelings of summer yet revel in the fact that summer has gone. It seems at peace with itself, glorying in the moment, basking in completion, celebratory. It's as if it is aware of the decay that will soon be implemented, yet determined to indulge in the sunshine of what is.

A buzzard circles overhead, quite low, crying; perhaps it is one of this year's chicks. The sun is hot, but from time to time a cool breath of air pushes in through the window. It is full of ozone, and you want to take it deep into your lungs. Initially, it seems the same as those spring breezes – it is the same temperature, has the same strength – but the two are quite different. In spring there is urgency and the promise of warmth, of sun, of growth. A small shudder, a reminder that, though this is a perfect day, soon things will change. I want to go out and feel the sun on my face, turn away and feel it on my neck. The breeze picks up, the air is full of insects, but on one gust a few noisy ash leaves rattle to the ground.

The hot borders have reached their peak, and this is just the right sort of day to take them in. Everything has come together. Rudbeckia, heleniums, big clumps of crocosmia are all blazing away. The round, bronzed leaves of the cotinus are fully extended and repeated down the border. The big, bold leaves of tropical plants lend a touch of panache, and vivid red dahlias zing out from the jungly background.

Monday 20 September

Our onions this year are a bit on the small side, but perfectly formed! They are solid and I want them to keep well, so I'm pegging them out on the strings in between our bean poles. This way they get the maximum air and sunshine. I must remember to bring them in, though, just like the washing, if it starts to rain.

Wednesday 22 September

The tomatoes in our little greenhouse are extremely fruitful, and so far, fingers crossed, there's no sign of blight. They are easy to pick, too, with this new way of supporting them – canes tied into the apex of the greenhouse roof. Since I'm growing them all as cordons, every few days I go along removing any new shoots from the leaf axils. This concentrates all the plants' energies on flowering and producing fruit. Despite my best intentions, I always seem to miss a few and find a renegade shoot or two heading for the roof. I allow about six trusses of tomatoes to develop per plant before stopping it at the top. With the bounty of this year's crop, Neil has already started to fill the freezer with home-made passata and minestrone.

OPPOSITE *Ornamental gingers are magnificent plants. This is Hedychium coccineum 'Tara', Tony Schilling's seedling named to honour his daughter.* BELOW *Sylvie loves sleeping.*

There are a few plants that wait until now to make an exhibition of themselves. Earlier copious rain coupled with the Indian summer we're just enjoying have encouraged them to put on an even more spectacular show than ever, and their bold foliage and vivid flowers are setting the garden ablaze. It's true there is already drama from huge heleniums – perennial sunflowers from the prairies of North America that make he-man clumps at the back of the border – alongside imposing stands of fennel filling in every available space with its filigree foliage. But both are elbowed to one side by the towering columns of more exotic subjects: cannas, hedychiums and bananas. All have broad, paddle-shaped leaves hugging bold stems, and outlandish flowers.

Cannas are familiar plants, often used in municipal plantings; they can look like stranded scarecrows in a sea of petunias. But give them their head amongst other show-offs and drama queeens and their talent shines out; they become leading ladies, stars of the show, and their flowers are a wow. Even with our warmer winters, cannas are not hardy. When frost blackens the foliage I'll chop off the soggy leaves, dig up the tubers, roots and all, get rid of excess soil and store them under the greenhouse staging. Those in pots will be moved indoors too. Next spring I'll wake them up, pot them up in loam-based compost, and give them light, air, warmth and water.

Ginger lilies, or hedychiums, do not need quite so much cosseting to give an equally outstanding show. They come from the foothills of the Himalayas, their foliage is as lush as that of cannas but always green. The flower spikes are extraordinary; there may be as many as twenty or thirty on every one, each with a long corolla tube and a protruding stigma which is evidence of the major difference between them and their canna cousins – scent. This perfumed paraphernalia is all in aid of pollination by moths; the scent is almost overpowering as dusk descends. In common with cannas, though, they have extensive rhizomatous roots, so rather than lift them each autumn, I leave them in the ground and usually heap soil over their roots. After this, the bed looks as though it has been visited by giant moles, but as long as the mounds are big enough, the rhizomes won't freeze. Last winter – the hardest for many years – I left my gingers unprotected, but most have survived and those I brought out from the greenhouse in July are flowering resplendently.

Hedychium 'Assam Orange' took up residence in our hot beds four or five years ago and is at the zenith of its performance right now. It has narrow spikes of flower composed of scores of small, vivid orange flowers. When it comes to perfume, though, *Hedychium gardnerianum* is the most exotic. It can have as many as thirty blossoms to a spike; the pale, creamy yellow flowers open in succession and big red stamens push forward and announce their presence. If I miss the visual broadcast, for sure I'll be stopped in my tracks by the scent. I've been known to get up in the middle of the night to go outside and enjoy the perfume by moonlight.

Monday 27 September

I've been sowing loads more salad crops; ideally I should do this every couple of weeks, but sometimes I lapse. We love Chinese greens, but I'm a sucker for lettuce. I have a packet of Italian mixed lettuce seed, 'Misticanza di Lattughia', which I have been sowing for years, there are enough seeds in the packet to feed a small town. Some are soft and round-leaved, some crisp and crunchy, some have red leaves, some green. I cut them, and they come again.

Wednesday 29 September

Looking at new plants makes me think about my gardening journey. When you first start so much is unknown, so much totally new, and everything half frightening, half exhilarating. Ever since I can remember, I've wanted my own garden. When I was little, my mum gave me a strip of garden where I could grow whatever I wanted. It was full of straightforward flowers – marigolds and nasturtiums. Later I experimented with freesia bulbs, planting them in the black soil (tantamount to gardening on coal), in the shade of the big Victorian semi where we lived at the time. Needless to say, they never produced the beautiful scented flowers I'd seen on the packet.

But in the same place me and my mum had success with a beech hedge, which eventually divided our narrow front garden from the A6. It was composed of tiny seedling beeches that I'd dug up on a visit to North Wales. When Neil and I lived in Ladbroke Grove, London, our landlord allowed me to grow plants in half of the front garden, which was north facing with no direct sunlight at any time. There were plants given to me by Charlie the milkman, and others rescued from demolition sites, including a magnificent *Dracunculus vulgaris*, a dragon arum. Our landlord didn't approve of that; not only does it have a foul smell, but also a creeping habit. It tunnelled under the garden path and came up on his side too. Meanwhile, every night after I'd planned my lessons for the next day (I taught art in White City), out would come the gardening books and I'd steep myself in pictures and descriptions of a world of plants. One day, when there was no school, I heard Roy Lancaster on *Woman's Hour* and was completely hooked. Then more than ever, I yearned to know more about plants and how to grow them. I taught in a boys' school and every so often would take a whole class to Kew Gardens to draw and take photographs as references for their artwork. It wasn't altogether altruistic. Our trips were halted at one stage, though, when two of my boys went for an unauthorised row in the boat that the gardeners used for maintaining the pond – Dean McGillicuddy and Mark Carter, your time is up, come in please.

I've been so fortunate to be involved with plants and the people who love them for the last thirty years or more. There are new people to meet and new plants too, all the time. Aren't I lucky?

September
Rudbeckias

OPPOSITE *Using a plant
intermittently throughout
an area leads the eye on
through the space,
boundaries disappear
and a feeling of distance
is created.*

Sometimes I wonder whether there is too much rudbeckia in my garden. Then on a gloomy late September day, when the golden flowers of *Rudbeckia fulgida* var. *deamii* light up the murky depths like so many burning torches, I almost wish there were even more.

Most rudbeckias are from the plains and prairies of the USA, in common with the autumnal asters, the Michaelmas daisies, which accompany them. They are straightforward plants that need no fuss or cosseting. Most will endure for years without any attention, although it only seems fair to reward such stalwart performers by dividing them occasionally and planting them in fresh soil in a different venue. Alternatively, plants can be fed in situ with a good mulch of rotted manure or home-made compost. In both cases we discard the old woody centres of the clumps. Most rudbeckias need no staking; their stems are strong and their constitution robust. All through the summer they wait quietly in the wings, biding their time until they get their chance to shine.

Rudbeckias are all predominantly yellow daisies often called black-eyed Susan for their dark, conical centres. There are annuals splashed with mahogany, double-flowered forms too, but it is the most simple that make a lasting impression. *Rudbeckia fulgida* var. *deamii* is numero uno.

Flowering at its usual time, a few clumps or even one large plant of *Rudbeckia fulgida* var. *deamii* can create a feeling of ease, as though summer would last indefinitely. It is an archetypal 'Indian summer' plant. Towards the end of summer, each bushy plant has finished its construction phase, and there is a green lull before the yellowness gets going. Branches and stems pause, buds swell. The pointed, green calyces open into green stars, the back of the petals, slender and green, are revealed. They broaden and stretch, resting on the plateaux provided by the calyces. At this stage I run out daily to inspect them, anxiously anticipating the first flash of yellow. Once it starts, given even a modicum of sunshine, flower follows glorious flower until the whole plant glows. At its height there are so many flowers, so much yellow, you can hardly see its leaves. Left to its own devices it will keep going in all directions, just as it would have done on its native prairies, making vast explosions of yellow.

Some gardeners are snooty about yellow. I used to be one of them. Even before I started gardening I was off yellow. As a fine-art student I arbitrarily decided to give yellow a miss for a whole year until I was told, rather pointedly, that yellow was the colour of spirituality. By this argument *Rudbeckia fulgida* var. *deamii* must be one of the most spiritual of plants. Its flowers are certainly among the most yellow of yellows. The colour of their golden discs is made all the more intense by black, velvety centres, opening in huge abundance during early autumn and continuing in succession until its end. In some years they go on glowing into the first murky days of winter, and the black central cones persist long after that, making bobbly thickets among sere grasses.

Their flowers are favourites with butterflies and other pollinating insects and finches feast on their seedheads.

The Hot Bed

Fruition and fullness suits these beds most. Flowerheads and grasses will be left as far into the winter as possible. In spring the structure of the garden is dominant, but paths and edges are softened by pots of tulips. In late May and early June the first blatant blast in the hot borders is sounded by big, red poppies, and from then on it's a carefully orchestrated free-for-all.

October

As autumn progresses, the kaleidoscopic range of colour within our gardens begins to change. It's like a watercolour where paint has been applied in the first place with a range of bright colours, each dab and stroke distinct from the last until now, when a giant brush descends; a soft and loving brush that washes over the whole picture, bringing the colours closer and into intimate contact with each other. Edges become more indistinct and colour more muted, nothing shouts or clamours, all is warm, rich, mellow.

At this time of year it would be difficult for anyone, except perhaps a determined colour iconoclast, to make things clash. But the lack of colour extremes throws other factors to the forefront: texture, pattern and scale all take on greater significance. Movement, too, and sound play leading roles as the autumn progresses. It is difficult to depict such elements, but that is where your imagination comes into play. The whisper of lilting grasses swaying in the breeze, the rustle of leaves in the high branches as it changes to a crunchier, more abrasive sound, warning of their imminent descent.

OPPOSITE *This is one of my favourite views of the garden as October begins. The seat is so welcoming, the plants warm and mellow.*

There is a visual rhythm, too, that is running through the plants. There are melodies, crashing crescendos and quiet pauses and the pizzicato of oft-repeated plants. Growth is past its zenith and from now on plants will start to diminish; the garden withdraws gradually.

One of the most engaging aspects of gardening is watching the ebb and flow within an area as plants grow and change. Though our hot borders have been full of shooting stars – giant red poppies, dahlias and their ilk – the majority of plants within the adjacent brick garden have long seasons, making a contribution from the first magical days of spring through till winter. Autumn daisies, though, have their special time; though their earlier foliage and flower buds lent structure and weight to the planting, it is now that they come into their own. Clouds of blue with high notes of chrome and lemon-yellow in cadences create a feeling of abundance perfectly in tune with ripening apples and the heady scent of sun-kissed blackberries.

With memories of summer fading fast and autumn well ensconced, it is sometimes easy to forget what a brilliant month October can be. As leaves colour up for their final fling, the garden is still rich in floral treats, and with a short spell of sunny weather the autumn-hatched butterflies have been out and about. There have been dragonflies and hoverflies aplenty, and the plant that so many have plumped for as their first-choice landing stage is *Helianthus* 'Lemon Queen', an epic perennial sunflower loaded with big, yellow, dark-eyed daisies. Even on a dull day this bank of cheery flowers brightens up the whole garden. Fothergilla and cercidiphyllum are beginning to glow with rich autumnal colour.

But even the distractions of late flowers and blushing foliage with all its glorious ambers, russets and reds, cannot dispel the melancholy that begins to haunt the garden.

SATURDAY 2 OCTOBER

We planted our crab apple, *Malus* 'Golden Hornet', thirty years ago. It was a spindly stick, with a few small branches sticking out, and it was bare – bare roots, bare trunk, bare branches. It must have been November when we brought it home along with a small collection of other special trees and shrubs from the old Veitch's nursery, outside Exeter. They all travelled unceremoniously in the back of our old Land Rover. I was nervous at that stage about planting anything that didn't arrive in a pot, but I did what all the books told me – prepared the ground well, and duly planted the tree. I had already built a wall beneath the spot where it was to live and it took pride of place on the corner overlooking the track and what was to become Annie's garden. There was no Annie then. What a different place the garden looked all those years ago.

What a bonus – days of glorious sunshine, autumn leaves drifting down in leisurely fashion and crunching underfoot, wafty grasses glowing golden,

moving gently to and fro on an occasional draft of warm air. One of the major reasons for jubilation is that there are extra days to gather in the harvest. Not just squashes and beans – the harvest that's all important to me is the seed harvest. When we first came here, I wouldn't have dreamt of collecting seed. I believed that, to stand any chance of germinating, seed had to come in a brightly coloured packet from a garden centre or supermarket shelf. But after watching plants self-seeding around the garden, it dawned on me that the seeds they set must be viable and that it might be possible to emulate them by sowing their seed myself to produce new plants. I've no idea how many plants I've grown here from seed over the last thirty years, but it must be quite a few. One of the greatest joys is that even the most unusual of plants often set seed, meaning we can make more and share them.

Each year there is something new and different to try, and in some years there are particular groups of plants, or plant families, that I seem to home in on. One of my favourites is Apiaceae, the umbel family. They are such gracious plants, many with finely cut, ferny foliage and handsome plateaux of tiny flowers. In a dry spell a few weeks ago, I collected seed from pimpinella, a pretty umbel with pale-pink flowers, and sowed it there and then. Not only did it germinate rapidly, but the plants are now big enough to be pricked out. Sheila, who works with us, put them into individual modules and they are growing away happily. *Angelica archangelica*, sown at the same time, has grown so well that each seedling needed its own small pot. Both will keep growing right through the winter.

So today I'm collecting seed from *Bupleurum longifolium*. It too is an umbel, but it doesn't look like one. Each flower, and there are several to every head, looks like a brown bouquet with a collection of seeds surrounded by papery bracts. I will store half the seed in a paper bag over the winter, and sow it in spring, but the rest I'm sowing today.

THURSDAY 7 OCTOBER

Every season has its own smells. In October you're expecting the smell of ripe fruit, wood smoke and damp earth. At this time of year, though, I make a detour to one of the lower beds, just in front of the oak fence, to smell something special. As I turn off the track, the air is full of perfume, but a strange perfume; it's a warm, friendly aroma, just like toffee apples. It's coming from two cercidiphyllum planted yards away. As temperatures drop and their beautiful heart-shaped leaves turn to gold, their perfume is released. Since there are seven cercidiphyllum in the garden (I'm rather keen on them), you can enjoy this perfume almost everywhere. They provide a double treat, because on cold mornings in autumn they emit the same perfume as they do in the spring when their leaves first appear.

Mind you, the cercidiphyllums weren't my real destination. What I've really come to enjoy is the perfume of *Actaea racemosa*, one of the most elegant

Life in a Cottage Garden

members of the buttercup tribe. Not only are its looks appealing, with tall spires of pure white flowers wafting elegantly in the October sun, but their scent is beguiling. Many members of ranunculaceae are long-lived plants, hellebores, peonies and aconites amongst them. My actea has lived in this bed for at least ten years and shows no sign of deteriorating. Quite the opposite; it gets better and bigger year by year. There are perennials which just seem to grow in stature.

SUNDAY 10 OCTOBER

When I'm choosing herbaceous perennials, I seldom consider their eventual autumnal garb as a reason for selecting them. Given that a plant will fit the soil and situation, I'm more interested in how it will perform at the height of its display rather than how it will look when it is on the wane. Flower form and colour have priority and leaves are equally important – they last for much longer too. But there is an extra act in the production and the garden reminds me now how important this is. In some cases foliage goes through dramatic changes as the year starts to ebb.

The huge heart-shaped leaves of hostas turn slowly to soft yellow, outlining their shape; gradually nature gilds the leaves entirely. Hostas are close relations of lilies, and another branch of the same family, the Convallariaceae, also turn to gold now. Lily-of-the-valley, alongside its mouth-wateringly scented sprigs of flower in spring, has fine twin leaves, green and fresh then but now transformed to gamboge. Solomon's seal is taller, structural, and its broad, ribbed leaves decorating elegant arching stems change to a similar warm colour. An American relation, *Smilacina racemosa,* does much the same thing as day length shortens.

Many of the herbaceous plants in Alice's garden are members of the rose family. Taller species, including meadowsweets and astilbes, draw attention to themselves again now. Their flowering may have finished long ago but providing I leave them to do their thing, their seedheads make a fine display above foliage that changes through yellows, reds and russets.

Rodgersias are prized for their boldness. For any garden with substantial soil on the damp side they add drama and panache. The bold palmate leaves of *Rodgersia pinnata* 'Superba' are often red when they emerge, turning green during summer, when the leaves expand upwards and outwards, and becoming deep, plummy red as the days shorten. The leaves look lacquered or polished, as though each one had received an extra rub over. The flower panicles too are admirable, up to 3ft high, and stand proud of the foliage, lasting deep into the winter. Under the crab apple the huge leaves of *Astilboides tabularis* become even more conspicuous late in the season. Its leaves make perfect inverted parasols, full of crab apples now, and are flushed with red and orange before their demise. All autumn colour is a sign of imminent expiration, which makes it all the more poignant.

OPPOSITE *Alice's garden is in its most reflective mood now. Most of the pink and crimson has faded, and the once bright-green leaves are tawny now.*
ABOVE Lysimachia clethroides *acquires a new persona in its autumn garb.*

TUESDAY 12 OCTOBER

Leaves are wondrous organisms. They ingest carbon dioxide and pump out oxygen and water, but even when the chlorophyll that they so magically produce breaks down and they fall to the earth, they continue adding use, making a vital contribution to the life of a garden. The brilliant autumn colour we witness (it is particularly dazzling this year) is a result of this process. As the tree shuts down for winter, responding to cooler temperatures and shorter daylight hours, the chlorophyll disappears; the pigments that were always there underneath the green layer, get their opportunity to shine. Physically, in terms of bringing life to the tree, the leaves have served their purpose. The cambium layer seals off the stem to protect it from the ensuing cold, the bond between leaf and tree is broken and it falls to the ground along with all its brethren leaves.

On streets, in fields and woods, layers of leaves carpet the ground, children frolic through them and keepers of perfect lawns curse them. In Japan leaves are treasured aesthetically as much after they have fallen as they were when they decorated the branches. Their renewal and decay are the best illustration of the cyclical nature of gardening.

FRIDAY 15 OCTOBER

Because Fifi has proved to be such a bundle of energy, our walks with the dogs have got longer. Trundling through the fields and walking down the lanes, we are immersed in the changes that take place day by day. Of course we notice much more when it's not pouring down with rain. Today is quiet, with low cloud, and the light dissipates colour, affording a chance to assess it, to measure where the season has reached. The bracken in the hedgerow is all turned to rust. The gnarled oaks at the corner of Pool Lane and those scattered through the surrounding fields are not just brushed with yellow, close up you can pick out subtle nuances – gamboge, amber and ochre. You could use up your whole vocabulary of yellow and still be nowhere near including the gamut of colour within just a few leaves. To think those colours have been there hiding all season.

The colour of beech leaves is much more vivid, more strident than those of oak, and their leaves fall to the ground much more rapidly. In the nearby Crooked Oak Valley, which, as you'd expect is full of oaks, there is often colour through to December, whereas the beech trees that hug our garden will long have been bare. Why do hawthorns lose all their leaves yet retain their berries so magically? Their twiggy iron-grey branches are hung with countless dark crimson higs. Is it an invitation to the redwings, who have just started to wend their way south, to come and eat, perhaps? Even where the hedgerows have been hacked, solitary hawthorns stand proud of their more lowly neighbours.

Life in a Cottage Garden

TUESDAY 19 OCTOBER

Most of the seed I grow is sown in seed trays or pots. Occasionally in the case of biennials plants like foxgloves, wallflowers and sweet Williams, I will sow their seeds directly into the ground, often at the edge of one of the vegetable beds. When the seedlings are big enough they are transplanted with a few inches between each plant, but within a year they will have been planted in their final positions. Because berries and nuts sometimes take an age to germinate, I'm building a separate bed to sow them in. It's a wooden box the size of a Dutch light, placed directly onto one of the veg beds where I've already improved the soil with leaf mould, sand and grit. There are spare Dutch lights on the nursery that I can borrow to cover the bed in really frosty or very wet weather.

THURSDAY 21 OCTOBER

Raking up leaves is one of October's gentlest pastimes. As the trees in the garden grow bigger each year, there is more and more of it to do. It gives you an opportunity to see how plants in the surrounding beds are doing – some of them have been out of my consciousness since the spring. It also provides the garden with one of its most important benefits. Barrowfull by barrowfull, leaves are carted off to the leaf-mould heap. It's just four posts with pig wire stretched between them. It's big. It will take them a year or two to break down, but it's an ongoing process. There's always rich, dark leaf mould to be fed back to the garden. As I tumble the leaves onto the heap, I can feel the pattern of the year impressing itself on the earth.

SATURDAY 23 OCTOBER

It seems a shame to pick too many of the glowing red berries of *Viburnum opulus*, the guelder rose, they are so seductive with evening sunlight shining through them. Blackbirds love them, and since they are growing close to an old abandoned blackcurrant that still bears fruit abundantly, this corner has become a favourite haunt. If a plant you've grown from a berry becomes a tree or a shrub, a permanent feature in the garden, you may go on to develop a lifelong friendship. Growing trees from seed you have collected is a wondrous experience, whether it's a single specimen or a stretch of native hedge.

It may be gratifying, but it is not necessarily quick, nor foolproof. There are simple steps, though, to help berries, nuts and assorted tree seeds to germinate readily. Stratification sounds very technical, but as with all aids to propagation it emulates a natural process. Nature always allows for a high degree of failure. If every hig on each hawthorn tree became a new tree, we would be inundated, but very few will ever become trees in their own right.

OPPOSITE *There'll be no shortage of work for weeks and I'll still be raking leaves in November. It's enjoyable though – it doesn't feel like work.*
BELOW *The guelder rose,* Viburnum opulus, *could hardly contribute more. Heads of exquisite white flowers in spring are followed by vigorous green leaves which turn red in autumn, accompanied by translucent red berries.*

OPPOSITE *The sea-green lichen covering the cercis will last as long as the tree. The leaves of the cercis and of the surrounding trees will fall, the garden will die back, but* Aconitum carmichaelii *icarries on.*

BELOW *Surely the best, certainly the boldest, of all climbers in autumn guise has to be* Vitis coignetiae.

When trees are grown from seed we can offer each one customised care. The embryo in every seed contains an inhibitor that prevents the seed germinating until the time is right. This is usually when the weather starts to warm up after a prolonged period of cold; in other words, after winter and into spring. It is a bio-chemical change that takes place, rather than a physical one. By replicating this same process in a controlled environment, not only can I maximise the seed's chance of success but the whole process can be telescoped into a shorter time period. The easiest process is to plant the seeds in the open ground after collection, but in mild winters temperatures may not be cold enough for long enough to ensure the seed germinates the following spring. The answer is to provide your own winter by chilling the seed. Mix seed with four times its volume of sieved damp leaf mould (peat always used to be recommended for this) and put the lot into a polythene bag – you can add coarse grit if it seems too cleggy. Label and leave in the warm for a couple of days whilst the seeds absorb enough moisture to make them swell, then put the bag in the coldest bit of the fridge for two months.

Seeds have many idiosyncracies, but for simplicity's sake this is a general practice that can be adopted and which will work for most seeds, including my viburnum berries. When they come out of the fridge I'll sow them into my newly prepared seed bed where I've already worked in leaf mould – it contains the fungi which are an essential element in healthy tree growth, forming complex symbiotic relationships with the roots.

WEDNESDAY 27 OCTOBER

For me, October is the most atmospheric of months. It has its own pace, its own rhythm; contemplative and sometimes wistful. It's the time we look back in our gardens. It's a season to indulge in and enjoy. Though I know it can't last forever, on golden days I never want it to end.

Its subdued colour palette is unique. You are especially aware of it because the biggest inhabitants in the garden are the ones that change most tellingly. It is during October, even more than they did in May, that the trees take over and become the focus of attention.

The garden is at its most earthy now and there is a dynamism in it that is just as powerful as that of spring. The noise of shoots retracting, stems withering, leaves falling, has a deep under-rhythm as roots, tubers and bulbs draw down strength and energy into the dark, rich soil.

The constant change and the awareness this provides of the massive cyclic power of nature could never be enjoyed in more tropical climes.

For some it's difficult to enjoy gardens at this time of year – there is nothing fresh and zingy. But spring and summer are the times for all that razzamatazz. The retina-searing reds and vivid oranges of high summer are long gone, colour now is mellow and warm. It seeps into the consciousness. All is quieting down. The change is inexorable; it's time to surrender.

October
Asters

OPPOSITE Aster
cordifolius x 'Little
Carlow', with clouds of
simple blue daisies on tall,
branching stems and glossy
leaves is the tops. It is the
best of mixers, perfectly
at home with the
brilliant chrome-yellow
of rudbeckia.
BELOW Spangled through
our wet and windswept
garden are stars of blue.
One of the best is Aster x
frikartii 'Mönch'. Its
simple, single flowers, with
their rays of slender petals,
are beyond compare.

September 29th is Michaelmas Day, traditionally one of the hiring days for farm workers and the day that gives its name to one of our most familiar autumn flowers. Close to the railway, on my way back from Barnstaple, is a piece of waste ground where each year clouds of white and blue take over. Across the narrow road is a row of cottages, and almost certainly, long ago, one of the inhabitants cleared these Michaelmas daisies from their plot and chucked them out onto the waste ground. Their loss was our gain, their swathes of dainty stars lift the spirits, flowering from Michaelmas right through October. I can remember the same phenomenon on Manchester bomb sites when I was little, where huge patches of these daisies, together with tall, vivid yellow helianthus, would take over. Such tenacious flowers are so welcome; when you see their opportunism and will to live, you are reminded of their origins on the prairies of North America.

Our asters of the moment at Glebe Cottage are those with clouds of small flowers creating a cumulus effect in different parts of the garden. Most are close to species, which means not only do they have a wild and wayward look that fits in with the feel of the garden, but they are disease-free, which accords with our organic ethos. The best of the lot is *Aster cordifolius* x 'Little Carlow'. Its small daisies are so tight-packed that the leaves and stems are invisible. There is a small seat on a brick platform which is surrounded by this plant and it is a treat to sit there and watch insects gathering pollen and feasting on the nectar. When the sun shines they are visited by flotillas of autumn-hatched butterflies – red admirals, peacocks and tortoiseshells. Neil's bees love this aster too, and they feed on it until late in the day, when its clouds of blue flowers take on an extra intensity and depth of colour.

The common name for *Aster cordifolius* is wood aster; it still frequents the woodland edges of large parts of north-eastern USA. This makes it a perfect plant for awkward areas in shade. It's a lovely idea to think of a flower from the wild woods of the United States lighting up a backyard in Bognor, or a suburban space in Solihull or, come to that, a cottage garden in Devon.

Another favourite daisy here is *Aster divaricatus*. It makes dense tuffets of leaves from which branching wiry stems rise during the summer. The stems arch over gracefully until, just as it seems the mass of their flowers will weigh them down, they seem to 'set' and stay as though they had been sprayed with hair lacquer. The starry flowers are carried gracefully.

If this aster is diaphanous, *Aster lateriflorus* var. *horizontalis* is anything but. This does just what its name says, with straight uprights and right-angled laterals. Its dark stems are covered with a multitude of narrow, beetrooty leaves and embossed with tiny white daisies with maroon middles. In the winter it presents a very different persona, and though its scaffolding structure is maintained until next year, its colour bleaches out to sepia.

Michaelmas daisies epitomise October. See them and you can almost hear the crunch of crisp fallen leaves underfoot and smell the bonfire smoke. You wish the autumn would never end.

Life in a Cottage Garden

THE UPPER WOODLAND GARDEN

Some of the best-colouring autumn shrubs and trees live in this part of the garden, amongst them a pendulous cercidiphyllum and Fothergilla Monticola Group — *a witchhazel relative. Both are also spectacular in the spring when the fothergilla is crowded with fluffy catkins. The paths and routes around this series of small beds are easiest to see in winter, and though snow obliterates all detail, it simplifies the overall geography.*

Life in a Cottage Garden

11

November

As November begins, the season changes, sometimes almost imperceptibly, sometimes dramatically. There may be weeks when all you are aware of is a slow slide; colour becoming diluted slightly day by day as though slowly and steadily, drip by drip, more water was being added to Nature's paint palette. Colour seeps out, gradually draining away. At every time of year the garden has its own special beauty, and the absence of colour, foliage and flowers means the shape and architecture of the plants that remain can be seen more sharply and can be appreciated in their own right. For the most part these are woody plants, shrubs and trees.

Although I grieve as the last of the beech leaves float gently to the ground, their trunks and branches are exposed in all their iron-grey glory, the intricate framework of their branches revealed. There are more opportunities now to see through plants to new views and vistas. The apple tree is still laden, though its fruits hang from a bare scaffolding. Trunks and branches show off their structure and texture, enriched by lichen, moss and sometimes evergreen ferns. The garden's poetry becomes more textural. The great

ABOVE *All bulbs are intriguing, but those of Fritillaria imperialis are amongst the most arresting, with their thick scales and hollow centres.* OPPOSITE *The beginning and the end of November can be very different. At its best it invites you into the garden, with golden grasses swaying seductively.*

Life in a Cottage Garden

leaves of astilboides, crinkled and crumpled now, hang like so many long-abandoned Tibetan prayer flags. The arching stems of Solomon's seal, translucent in the low sun, reveal the patterns of their erstwhile life – mid-ribs, veins laid bare.

One day all is mild, mellow, autumnal, the next a thick frost envelops not only the garden but all the fields that surround it. Suddenly it is degrees colder. It is crisp, the grass white as white, the cold persists and gets into your boots, inside your gloves. Up by the top hedge two red deer stand in the sunshine, smudges of warm terracotta in a sea of shivering white against a sky of peerless blue. Only when the sun is at its highest do its low rays make green patterns on the grass. In the shadows of the hedges and trees it stays white all day. Then, just as you're lulled into a sense that time has almost come to a standstill, winter announces itself with a resounding crash.

Early next morning a north wind bursts into the garden. Everything has changed again; the trees are thrashing, wailing, the whole garden moves. Now the leaves don't fall of their own volition in their own time, they are torn from the trees and dashed to the ground. The sad but lyrical cadence of November's early melodies is pushed aside, bullied out of the way by deep clashes of cymbals, rumbling drums and the ominous thunder of winter.

Friday 5 November

Just as the leaves are falling – now, in fact – is the best time for taking hardwood cuttings, what's more, they won't take up any room in my greenhouse. Space in there is at a premium in November.

I'm taking cuttings now from several straightforward shrubs – elders, physocarpus and viburnum – plants I want more of, both for the garden and to add to various hedges. This is one of the cases where it pays to think ahead. I try to remember to prune in the previous year anything I've got my eye on for hardwood cuttings. Hard-pruning induces vigorous new growth which, when it matures in November, makes excellent material.

I take strong stems from the shrubs I've chosen; I'll cut long stems into pieces and make several cuttings from each one; they need to be about 6–8 inches long. I've already dug a a short trench (and added sharp grit to the bottom of it) with one vertical wall, in a sheltered part of the garden, close to the side door, where my cuttings will be able to stay for a year or so. I'll push them in a few inches apart with two or three buds above soil level. The only exception to this is when I'm trying to produce a single-stemmed tree – in which case the whole cutting should be submerged with the top just below soil level. This will inhibit the lower buds from growing. I'll lean the cuttings against the wall and fill in the trench. They'll need very little attention apart from gently firming back the soil if it's been really frosty.

In a year's time the cuttings should have good roots and several side shoots and they can then be transplanted.

WEDNESDAY 10 NOVEMBER

Bulbs contain everything necessary to make a new plant, storing food and energy efficiently until conditions are right to send down roots, put out shoots and push up the bud hidden deep inside them until it opens as a glorious flower.

Soil or compost is the other part of the equation, plus for hardy bulbs a period of cold followed by rising temperatures and preferably plenty of gentle rain. Most of the wild ancestors of our cultivated tulips come from mountain ranges in central Asia. They are subject to periods of extreme winter cold and to hot, baking temperatures in the summer. Though many of the tulips that grace our gardens now bear little resemblance to their wild counterparts, having been lovingly bred and tended over centuries by generations of Dutch and English nurserymen, they still manifest the temperament of their untamed predecessors. Giving any plant the sort of environment and conditions it would experience in nature will help it feel at home and enable it to do its best.

As far as tulips go, that means providing excellent drainage, planting them in the sunniest spot available and planting them late – the later the better. In our increasingly mild, soggy winters, early-planted tulips are liable to start growing immediately, which means they are more subject to disease. At Glebe Cottage tulip planting has become a bit of a ritual. Nowadays we grow all our tulips in pots. Earlier attempts (and there have been many of them) to grow tulips in the open ground failed miserably – unless you count feeding the local mouse, vole and squirrel population as a success. Even tulips that have survived their depredations do not grow well, objecting to my heavy clay soil. So I plant them, lots of them, in big terracotta pots and to create as impressive a show as possible. I cram them in so they are almost touching and plant several pots of each variety. Tulips are amongst the showiest flowers there are, and to do cultivated tulips justice they need to be concentrated. All our pots are gathered together on the terrace where our main mouse-deterrents, Sylvie and Sylvester, our two cats, regularly patrol.

SUNDAY 14 NOVEMBER

Our polytunnels are once more covered in plastic and plants are beginning to look snug in their winter accommodation. Needless to say, it may have been too little too late for some of them. We've had frost. The dark-leafed banana, ironically a replacement for the one lost to the cold last winter, may survive, but at the moment it looks decidedly bedraggled.

When I carried it in it was almost too heavy to lift into the barrow, but after its predecessor's death I'm determined not to lose it. I'd forgotten just how many huge plants in pots I'd used in the hot borders during the summer. Many of them are hedychiums, and though their bright, scented

Life in a Cottage Garden

flowers and their gorgeous, bright green, paddle-shaped leaves are a memory now, their present incarnation, sepia and umber leaves and monochrome stems and flower heads, has its own eerie beauty. As they go into their winter quarters I chop off the stems at pot level – unless they still have some vestige of green, in which case they go into the greenhouse as they are to allow every bit of energy to return to the rhizomes. There are dahlias too, blackened and shrivelled by the frost. The canes that lent them support during their season of splendour are the most dominant feature. Their stems are still tied to them like ghosts unable to escape.

But why do I leave everything to the last minute? As the sun starts to drop below the horizon, choices have to be made, priorities adopted – what is the most important? What could manage? What would definitely die? Subjectivity creeps in – what do I love most? Pots full of the handsome *Eucomis* 'Sparkling Burgundy' are first on the list. Each has its own substantial clay pot sitting on one of the broad brick steps up to the front door. I take them two by two to the barrow and wheel them off to the shed. They'll be gently transferred into plastic pots of a similar size to spend the winter underneath the staging in the greenhouse – the clay pots are needed for more tulips.

It's hard to believe that it is that time of the year already. More eucomis, seedlings from the big mother plants, have already been potted up and the big square pots which they have vacated are ready for even more tulips. No frost forecast tonight, I'll have to carry on in the morning.

MONDAY 22 NOVEMBER

My mum used to love coming to visit us. As well as seeing her granddaughters and us, of course, she adored the garden and welcomed the opportunity to keep up with progress, discuss plans and help. She always got stuck in. As is the way with mums, she would never turn up empty-handed. She always brought piles of butties, shared at the field's edge when the girls and I went up to meet her after her long journey (she had always deliberately made five times too many sandwiches for herself and it became a ritual). There would be other gifts too; cakes, pies and puddings (we even had a song to accompany the grand entrance of the steamed-jam pud) – and there were plants. Most were divisions of perennials from her own garden, primulas, phlox and astilbe, and cuttings she had raised herself. Many are still in the garden at Glebe Cottage. How I love them. Occasionally, though, perhaps for a birthday or some special occasion, there would be something that she had bought.

Among these were two Japanese acers, *Acer palmatum* 'Osakazuki' and *Acer* 'Aconitifolium'. When she brought them and we planted them together, one at the top of the garden the other at the bottom, they were small and young; now they are mature. Each time I walk through the garden, either on my way out or coming home, I am twice reminded of her.

OPPOSITE *It's not until autumn that* Acer *'Aconitifolium' really comes into its own. Its divided leaves glow orange and you can see it from the top of the field.*
BELOW *Calendula seeds in the shed. I'll sow some of them this week to have strong plants for the spring.*

November
Molinia

Sometimes in my garden, despite careful planting,
everything looks too contrived – a stage set rather than somewhere that
happened naturally. But there are plants within it that save the day, whose
whole purpose in life seems to be to bring light and music to the proceedings
– not to mention a touch of frivolity. Grasses never take themselves too
seriously, they have the ability to move and sway, and in doing so they
orchestrate the garden, adding melodies, percussion, rustling and rattling
as they dance backwards and forwards, shimmering in the sun.

Grasses are creatures of the wind; they depend on it for pollination, it
rushes round them, through them, lifting them, bending them, making them
sway. Though there are grasses throughout the garden at Glebe Cottage, it is
in the brick garden and the hot beds that run along its length where they
really come into their own. Two grasses in particular, molinia and
hakonechloa, dominate here, and they are at their glorious best as November
starts. On quiet days plants of molinia stand around; they are planted in
groups, loitering on corners or standing in the midst of beds and borders,
tall and detached like a group of lads who can't think of anything to say. But
when the west wind blows, how they change – all trying to outdo one another,
animated, swashbuckling, no dawdling now.

Most of the molinias in this part of the garden are erect, *Molinia caerulea*
subsp. *arundinacea* cultivars 'Skyracer' and 'Windspiel' are tall and mobile.
Further down the garden the most elegant of all these purple moor grasses
wafts her graceful stems above the surrounding herbage. *Molinia caerulea* subsp.
arundinacea 'Transparent' is a late starter, only making a foot or so up until
May, but once it gets going there is no holding it back. From a cascading
clump of rather rough basal foliage, the flower stems begin to emerge in July.
At first the flowers stay tight packed around the main stem, but as this
lengthens they shake themselves free and the distance between the individual
flowers increases so that finally each tiny flower occupies its own separate
space. This open habit makes 'Transparent' one of the most graceful of all
grasses. Each flower glistens in the light, especially after a shower of rain.
Then the whole plant shimmers, each prism refracting light hither and
thither. As the flowers turn to seed, it becomes heavier and the stems arch
over gracefully, forming a series of arcs around the central clump of leaves.
Each stem can be 6 foot long.

What is striking about this plant is how dreamy it is despite its giant
proportions. Its airy form shows up in silhouette. Against a brilliant blue sky
it takes on a new dimension; against a dark backdrop, especially when it has
entered its golden autumnal phase, it is just as striking. All molinias go
through this metamorphosis. One of their most exciting facets is this gradual
transformation from green, blues and purples to straw and biscuit through
to glowing gold. Along with the fountainous hakonechloa and the fluffy silver
heads of miscanthus grasses, molinias turn the November garden into a place
of levity, movement and fun.

OPPOSITE Molinia
caerulea *subsp.*
caerulea *'Edith Dudszus'*
makes a series of
exclamation marks
amongst the fading clumps
of echinacea and asters.
BELOW Miscanthus
sinensis *has had several*
incarnations from soft,
silky and pink to silvery
and fluffy.

Life in a Cottage Garden

12

December

This is the darkest month; it is plunged into despair yet elevated by hope. December is a meaningful yet mysterious month. During its passage much will die, but before its end rebirth will start with an all-powerful upsurge. It is the time of the lowest ebb, the nadir. As the year moves towards the winter solstice and light decreases day by day, it's easy to feel cheated. The garden shuts down, creating a feeling of helplessness; its demise is inevitable and there is no point fighting – perhaps it is better to give in? It's tempting to scrape the mud from your boots and put them in the cupboard, but no, there is so much to do and December gardening has its own special pleasures.

Now comes the start of the big clean up. This may be the era of dying down, dying back, withdrawing, but underneath the surface of the soil so much is happening.

Sometimes the soil is crunch-cold, the wind is biting and the chances of having any meaningful interaction with the garden are below zero – so is the temperature. But there are still many jobs to do. Many of these anticipate the coming year, turning this month into a time of preparation; to

ABOVE *Neil always feeds the birds. The garden is full of them and their activity is a source of constant interest and amusement.*
OPPOSITE *Glebe Cottage in the mist through a hedge of fennel stems. The building is now 110 years old.*

Life in a Cottage Garden

retire to my shed and scan the boxes and baskets of paper bags full of seed that I've collected during the last few months is a treat to look forward to, then indulge in. Reading the names hastily scribbled, occasionally almost indecipherable, the image of those plants in their glory is conjured up. And as I winnow the seed, carefully separating it from the chaff and packing it into brown envelopes, the anticipation of all the plants these seeds will become is enough to carry me, smiling, through even the shortest, wettest day.

This is the season of mud and mire and mist. Pulling up the blind on some mornings it is difficult to see the garden – it seems to have disappeared during the night and drifted away. But the sun is there, although we may not see it; gradually the sky lightens and the beautiful beeches that safeguard the garden, wrapping it in their strong branches, emerge into view.

In the hazel woods close to the cottage, there is the smell of deer as you crush damp leaves and moss beneath your feet and watch your breath spread out in clouds before you. The scent is unmistakeable and all the signs are there: narrow paths where dainty hooves have cleft a way through the undergrowth, a few broken branches and snapped twigs where steaming, substantial bodies, many of them now in calf, have pushed through to strip moss and lichen from the ageing trunks.

The earth breathes. One enormous breath has been expelled and slowly, deeply, reassuringly, she breathes in once again.

Sunday 5 December

During December my time is shared between the inside and the outside. There are some years when the last month can be full of fine days. In December 1980, when Annie was a few months old, I remember feeding her in the morning, putting her into her pram and bringing her outside to sleep in the fresh air while I planted old roses and hellebores; the weather was mild and sunny.

We have had Christmas days when the girls stepped out without a single shiver in all their finery to take pictures, and Boxing Days when we took our first dog out to the beach and had to divest ourselves of scarves, gloves and even coats. There has been snow, fog and frost, and there was one year when we couldn't open the side door because of sheet ice – the ground was turned to tundra.

The shed and the greenhouse are always especially busy at this time of year. Although it is not a heated greenhouse, the soil-warming cables in the bench keep it frost-free. The greenhouse becomes a refuge for any plant which can't cope with plummeting temperatures or prolonged cold. There is never enough room, the bench affords new cuttings a flying start. Underneath it the floor is stacked with pot upon pot of semi-tender plants, bananas, hedychiums, dahlias, eucomis and canna. All on their winter vacation.

OPPOSITE *Cats always find the cosiest spots. As the windows steam up and the cold starts to bite, the first green shoots begin to appear, sometimes incubated by Sylvie and her twin brother Sylvester.* BELOW *Outside the garden shivers, but in tunnels, greenhouses and under coldframes, plants are tucked up for the winter.*

Plans are made now for the year ahead; it was this time last year when I started to think about how I would overhaul Annie's garden. The major work has been completed but there are still adjustments to make, fine-tuning to be carried out – and then before you know it, plants have grown away, increased faster than you could have imagined and it's time to think about it all over again. There is no beginning and no end to a garden, it is a set of processes, not a product.

This is what I love; this complex, interdependent evolution where you need to employ everything you have – experience, a little knowledge, craft, science, art and, wherever you can, a dash of poetry. Not to mention a lot of luck.

THURSDAY 9 DECEMBER

Not so very long ago, gardeners would have been straining at the bit to get out into their plots with their sharpest secateurs and most finely honed shears the moment autumn showed the first signs of changing into winter. Off they would go, slashing and chopping, reducing herbaceous borders to stubble. But times change, and so do gardening aesthetics, and consequently practices too. In the corner of our daughter Alice's garden are towering stems of a statuesque meadowsweet, *Filipendula ulmaria* 'Rosea'. In spring there were big clumps of fresh healthy leaves, in July the flowers atop stems at least a metre and a half tall began to make their fluffy pink froth. Now foliage has turned to russet and glowing orange, fading fast, the seed heads are intricate, branching formations, silhouetted against a blue sky. There is no point my pretending that I chose this plant for its seedheads, but now that I am treated to the sight of them I fall even more deeply under its spell. I could kick myself for what I've missed through my own over-zealous tidying in past years and how I've deprived the creatures who share the garden with me.

No more. Perhaps it's all to do with accepting a much more laissez-faire philosophy which has less to do with control and more to do with observing and enjoying what plants do, even on their way out.

Nowadays I always delay cutting back our perennial plants for as long as possible. Seedheads are an important source of food for birds, and since many stand so well for such a long time it would seem uncharitable to be too prompt about removing them prematurely. But it's not as altruistic as it sounds; seedheads make some of the best sculpture in the winter garden. Our blue-and-yellow garden, the brick garden, becomes a brown-and-brown garden during the winter months, but it is saved from descent into depression by a series of seedheads. The black cones of *Rudbeckia fulgida* var. *deamii*, stripped of its leaves, still make a graceful contribution above the elegant leaves of hakonechloa, dancing on as though no-one had told it the party was over. Fennel stems form a dramatic backdrop, towering high above the others. Some of the molinias have collapsed; one severe frost is enough to topple them, I'll catch them up in great bundles and take some into the house.

Life in a Cottage Garden

Monday 13 December

Nature's mechanisms are always intriguing, none more so than buds. In our temperate climate, the majority of our woody plants, trees and shrubs are deciduous. As winter approaches they drop their leaves, and at this time of year the new leaves that will replace them are just beginning to grow. Through them we will perceive the onset of spring. The way they swell and grow is subtle and almost imperceptible, yet inexorable.

Each bud contains in embryonic form leaves, stems and flowers, the whole of the year's growth, right up to the time when leaves and fruit fall to the ground next autumn.

What is the archetypal bud? A quick consensus of family and friends puts the horse chestnut at the top of the list. Certainly it evokes strong memories. I still have a drawing of the nature table I tended aged eight; in it a strong horse-chestnut twig in a jam jar takes pride of place, its sticky buds just beginning to burst. It is instantly recognisable, despite the childish technique, and immediately conjures up the delightful stickiness of the resinous scales.

Bud coverings are often sticky and tough, as in horse chestnuts, but sometimes the impervious scales that form the outer surface and protect the inner workings of a bud are astonishingly sheer. In late May, the track here alongside a forty-foot-tall beech hedge is ankle-deep in the fluff of pinky bronze leaf casings, cast off by buds as the first translucent leaves start to unfurl. They are soft, almost flippant.

In direct contrast, the chilly, charcoal-black buds of ash, hard and inpenetrable, make you wonder if they will ever break. Seemingly impervious to balmy spring weather, they remain petrified until at the last moment they swell suddenly and their starburst flowers issue forth.

As the buds of fruit trees begin to swell, there are already indications of the potential bounty of the crop. Looking up into the branches, even when silhouetted against a winter sky, the contrast between the slender leaf buds and the buxom round buds that contain the blossom is striking. The same goes for other woody members of Rosaceae: hawthorn and sloe, prunus and exochorda, whose orbicular flower buds earn it the name of pearl bush. Some shrubs are treasured for their buds as much as their flowers.

Sunday 19 December

I am always ambivalent about evergreens. Perhaps I prefer herbaceous perennials and deciduous trees and shrubs just because they're less predictable, because they have so many different personae, changing throughout the growing year, whereas the changes evergreens go through are subtle. True, they have flowers, berries sometimes and new growth, but somehow their basic personality is steady and dependable. Obviously it's not a failing on their part, but a shortcoming on mine.

OPPOSITE *The buds of* Magnolia stellata *demonstrate how beautiful the December garden can be even when colour is absent. You just want to caress the buds.*
BELOW *Trying out a borrowed power-washer to clean algae from the slippery bricks. It's a bit fierce.*

We are not overun with evergreens here, yet when I look objectively at my garden in December and try to imagine it without them, it would be a bare and barren place. The box hedge that squiggles its way through the hot borders is a must-have now; to think it was all grown from a few cuttings.

The white panicles of skimmia, although very much 'in the background' with their quiet, subtle demeanour, have scent you can smell long before you are aware of the shrubs. There are red berries, too, accompanying the flowers. There are bolder evergreens whose flowers are equally fragrant. *Mahonia japonica* is a classic winter shrub with an architectural presence, huge pinnate leaves and long, pendulous racemes of pale lemon flowers scented like lily-of-the-valley. Further up from my mahonia, on the east edge of the garden, are two camellias. They are not my favourite shrubs but they have both grown very strongly and are fine, healthy specimens. They have probably been there for twenty-five years or more. In spring they will be full of flowers but right now their foliage provides a smart and glossy show. They have the same texture, though not the same prickles, as the holly bushes higher up the hedge. These seem to be male and have never produced a berry, but a different self-sown bush of holly further down the garden is laden with berries this year. Another magical arrival along the same stretch of hedge is a delightful climbing rose with semi-double white flowers and glossy dark green foliage that seems to persist all year round. It has a few flowers even now, with a delicate perfume redolent of apples.

WEDNESDAY 22 DECEMBER

My garden overwhelms me. It fascinates me, intrigues me, absorbs me. Though I have known it for more than thirty years and have had a good deal to do with helping it to become whatever it is, it has secrets I do not pretend to understand – and possibly never will. Each part of it shows me new and often totally unexpected facets of the magical and mysterious – it is full of surprises.

When we came here I foolishly imagined I could somehow fashion it to my own design, impose myself and my will upon it, not in a controlling way, but somehow by subtle persuasion I thought I would meld the garden to my plan. Over the years I realised that it has such a strong spirit and such a sense of itself that it is the other way round. It has taught me how its plants grow, what they need, who they are. It has taught me to encourage plants to be themselves and it has taught me to consult it, to ask it what it wants to be and where it wants to go. It is a garden, and as such not a part of nature, but it is controlled by natural laws and as a gardener I must obey them. For once I submit.

When I look up from planting to the edge of the field, the beech trees are my inspiration. They guard the horizon, lifting their branches to the sky, collecting light and rain and giving praise to the goddess Mother Earth who gave birth to them and all the life on the planet.

The end is the beginning.

December
Holly & Ivy

December. Evergreens are steeped in folklore symbolising continuing life. They form a hugely significant part of the winter landscape. It's not just humans who have a soft spot for the holly and the ivy; this evergreen duo are two of the most important indigenous plants both in the wild and, by extension, in our gardens, for wildlife.

Perhaps the most obviously useful feature of the pair are the bright red berries of the holly. If you have ever been thwarted in your attempts to gather berry-rich holly by finding its branches stripped bare, you'll know only too well how much birds enjoy them. After all, that's why berries are as bright and juicy as they are. The maturing of the seed co-incides with the ripening of the berries and with a time when hungry birds are actively searching for food. On a scale of delectability, red berries are top-of-the-tree. Packed with sugars and protein, they are devoured by resident blackbirds and thrushes as well as flocks of visiting redwings and fieldfares.

These are a wonderful bonus for wildlife, especially when the plants, both male and female, have already provided a nectar treat for pollinating insects early in the year. Hollies are in flower in late winter and early spring when any kind of food is at a premium. The flowers are tiny, well-hidden amongst the prickly leaves, but both male and female flowers produce nectar – ambrosia for early insects. There are few on the wing at this time of year, but attracting them is essential, so a bargain is struck: insects get to eat and precious pollen is transferred. However, as each tree bears flowers of only one sex, to produce berries both male and female trees must be present.

Holly is a noble tree but if space is limited it will happily live its life as part of a hedge. Hedge trimming must be fairly relaxed, though, if there are still to be flowers and berries. Hollies withstand pollution and exposure well, unperturbed by traffic fumes or the salt-laden gales so prevalent in the winter at Glebe Cottage.

The common ivy, *Hedera helix* is the heroine of the wildlife garden. It too is a tough and tolerant plant. Sad to say it often has a bad press, sometimes being blamed for weakening walls. In fact, providing masonry is sound, ivy protects walls, drawing out damp. When ivy starts to climb and develop a woody trunk it begins to flower. Whilst it is creeping around on the ground no flowers are produced (although it does make wonderful cover for insects and small mammals). The intricate flower head is a masterpiece in symmetry and each of the flowers in the green and gold starburst is loaded with nectar, a vital source of food for late butterflies and other pollinating insects. It is the last port of call for foraging bees to make up crucial winter stores. When pollinated the flowers turn to black berries and in their turn these are vitally important for hungry birds who feast on them with relish. They mature over a long time so the larder goes on providing food for months.

Ancient religions attributed both holly and ivy with magical properties. Woe betide anyone cutting down a holly. Symbols of regeneration and continuing cycles in the midst of dark winter, they were revered.

Life in a Cottage Garden

Life in a Cottage Garden

1. Conservatory
2. Glebe Cottage
3. Owl box
4. Green Roof
5. Old greenhouse
6. Terrace
7. Beehive
8. Prunus padus
9. Cercis
10. Brick Garden
11. Magnolia stellata
12. Weeping Pear
13. Eleagnus `Quicksilver'
14. Acer 'Osakazuki'
15. Hot Beds
16. Copper
17. Weeping Cercidyphyllum
18. Cercidyphyllum twins
19. Prunus padus
20. Alice's Garden
21. Pergola
22. Cornus 'Norman Hadden'
23. Annie's Garden
24. Annie's apple tree
25. Crab apple
26. Woodland Garden
27. Stream
28. Magnolia 'Leonard Messel'
29. Nursery fence
30. Nursery
31. Apple 'Discovery'
32. Pond
33. Caravan
34. Acer 'aconitifolium
35. Way through to nursery
small greenhouse and
compost heaps

Index

Life in a Cottage Garden

Acknowledgements

First and foremost thanks to Jonathan Buckley for his fine work. I love my garden but it takes on new layers of meaning when seen portrayed in his outstandingly beautiful photographs. He seems to love the garden as much as I do and find it just as meaningful. Not one of the many grins on my face on the pages of this book was forced, I'd smile any time for Jonathan. Climbing ladders in a howling gale or plunging hands into icy soil for the umpteenth time are a pleasure when he asks you to do it — the outcome is always so worthwhile. Lorna Russell, our editor, is beyond compare, she is a star. Her enthusiasm for this book right from its inception has known no bounds, she has been endlessly encouraging, invariably optimistic and untiringly resourceful. Nothing has been too much trouble. It is true to say that without her actual help travelling vast distances, typing my words and prompting me to push on, it might never have arrived. Andrew Barron's design is sublime — and so elegant, yet you are never conscious of it. It does what all the very best designs do, enabling you to enjoy the book, pictures and words to their fullest without ever being conscious that a design has been imposed upon them. Thanks to Laura Higginson for all her work and Helena Caldon for last-lap organisation. Thanks Gordon for all your help at the initiation of this project. Grateful thanks to Peter Gibbs, weather-man extraordinaire for checking my generalisations and just for being so nice.

Working on the TV programme that this book accompanies has been a joy. Thanks Mark, David, Tim, Steve, Gerry, Gary, Jeremy, Neil and Simon. What a lovely programme we've made together and between us.

Thanks to all those who help in the garden and nursery with such love and enthusiasm especially Sheila, Barbara and Helen. Thanks to all my gardening friends constantly present in spirit here, the people are as important as the plants and make the place what it is. Special thanks to my lovely family, my mum who is ever-present and her grandaughters Annie, Alice and their dad Neil for enabling me to do what I do and more importantly for inspiring me to do it. And thanks to the garden, the most wondrous place there is.

This book is published to accompany the television series entitled *Gardener's World*, broadcast on BBC2 in 2011.

EXECUTIVE PRODUCER
Sarah Moors
SERIES PRODUCER
Tricia Lawton
PROGRAMME EDITORS
Neil Stacey and Simon Prentice

7 9 10 8

Published in 2011 by BBC Books, an imprint of Ebury Publishing. A Random House Group Company

TEXT
© Carol Klein 2011
PHOTOGRAPHY
© Jonathan Buckley 2011
MAP
© Neil Klein 2011

The Random House Group Limited Reg. No. 954009

Addresses for companies within the Random House Group can be found at www.randomhouse.co.uk

A CIP catalogue record for this book is available from the British Library.

ISBN 978 1 846 07871 2

COMMISSIONING EDITOR
Lorna Russell
PROJECT EDITOR
Laura Higginson
COPY-EDITOR
Helena Caldon
DESIGNER
Andrew Barron
MAP OF GLEBE COTTAGE GARDEN
Neil Klein
PHOTOGRAPHER
Jonathan Buckley
PRODUCTION
Antony Heller

The Random House Group Limited supports the Forest Stewardship Council® (FSC®), the leading international forest-certification organisation. Our books carrying the FSC label are printed on FSC®-certified paper. FSC is the only forest-certification scheme supported by the leading environmental organisations, including Greenpeace. Our paper procurement policy can be found at www.randomhouse.co.uk/environment

Colour origination by XY Digital
Printed and bound by Firmengruppe APPL, aprinta druck, Wemding, Germany

To buy books by your favourite authors and register for offers, visit www.randomhouse.co.uk